Being a refugee: learning and identity

a longitudinal study of refugees in the UK

Being a refugee: learning and identity

a longitudinal study of refugees in the UK

Linda Morrice

Trentham Books

Stoke on Trent, UK and Sterling, USA

Trentham Books Limited

Westview House	22883 Quicksilver Drive
734 London Road	Sterling
Oakhill	VA 20166-2012
Stoke on Trent	USA
Staffordshire	
England ST4 5NP	

First published 2011

British Library Cataloguing-in-Publication Data
A catalogue record for this book is available from the British Library

ISBN 978 1 85856 490 6

Cover photograph from iStock

Designed and typeset by Trentham Books Ltd
Printed and bound in Great Britain by 4edge Limited, Hockley

For Paul, Elena and Frankie with love

Contents

Acknowledgements

This book, and the research upon which it is based, has taken six years to come to fruition. However, the puzzles and curiosities which have driven the project took root many years ago while I was working with refugees and asylum seekers as an English for Speakers of other Languages (ESOL) tutor. I soon realised that the struggles to learn the idiosyncrasies of the English language were only a very small part of the learning and ongoing journeying in the lives of refugees. There is a much bigger story; there is a past, previous identities and ways of being; there are also dreams, aspirations and plans for the future. It was a desire to understand something about how this past, present and future become reconciled which brought me to this research. My deepest debt of gratitude is, therefore, to the refugees I have worked with over the years and who have shared their stories with me. In particular, the refugees whose life stories provide the foundation upon which this book is built. I have been profoundly moved, not only by their stories but also by the generosity and warmth they have shown me over the years. They have shared the highs and lows, the pain and joy of their lives, with courage, honesty and often humour.

I would like to thank my colleagues on the Education Doctorate programme at the University of Sussex: to Pat Drake, Louise Morley and John Pryor for their support and guidance as I picked my way through the academic landscape of Doctoral studies. Particular thanks are due to my academic supervisors; to Valerie Hey for encouraging me to use my sociological imagination and play with ideas, and to Judy Sebba for her enthusiasm for the subject matter and her forensic like attention to detail. I would also like to thank all of my colleagues, past and present, in CCE at the University of Sussex for their friendship, myriad insights and support. I am especially indebted to my friend and colleague, Pam Coare, for her belief, vision and tireless commitment to the cause of adult education and social equality. At a time when adult education is struggling to survive I have been sustained by the comradeship and encouragement of friends in SCUTREA (Standing Conference on University Teaching and Research in the Education of Adults) and my ex-colleagues in the WEA. In particular to my dear friend Wilma Fraser for her wisdom and solidarity.

Thanks are due to James Lee at the Refugee Council for trying to keep me up to date with developments in the ever-shifting policy world, and for agreeing to read some of the chapters (any errors or omissions, are of course, my own). I owe a debt of gratitude to Gillian Klein at Trentham Books for having the faith and confidence in this project. Most especially, I would like to thank and acknowledge the role of my family in enabling me to get to this point. To my parents, Alex and Joan Morrice, to my partner, Paul Norman, who has been unstinting in his encouragement and support during the writing process. Lastly, to my daughters, Elena and Frankie, who have always been welcome reminders that there are other things in life besides writing a book.

1

Refugee narratives

Introduction

This book tells the story of a group of people who become refugees. Combining life history and a longitudinal approach, we begin their narratives prior to migration, meeting them as people who had lives, families and communities. We then follow them from the point of arrival in the UK through their first five years in the UK and witness their hopes, dreams, anxieties and set backs as they seek to rebuild their lives.

Bauman (2004) has argued that refugees are the 'wasted lives' of globalisation, stripped of all identities but one – that of being stateless, statusless and functionless. Refugees do undoubtedly face enormous challenges. The label itself is both powerful and emotive, conjuring notions of loss, suffering and passive victims. The stories presented here are not those of passive victims, rather they are the stories of creative, resourceful people who are actively adapting to the new circumstances in which they are living. These are people managing to provide for themselves and their families in the UK and, more often than not, family members left behind in the country they have come from. They show how refugees resist the limiting social positioning and identities imposed by the asylum process, and how they struggle to negotiate the harsh conditions in the UK, to establish a legitimate and valued way of being and being seen. The stories illuminate the learning processes, the choices and pathways taken as they negotiate sustainable identities for themselves in a new social space, and they draw attention to the ways policy can restrict and hinder attempts to rebuild lives.

Refugees have to adjust to ruptures that unexpectedly modify the structure and the meaning of their lives as adults. Uprooted from former communities, culture, work and language, they are stripped of aspects of their previous identity. Previous ways of knowing and understanding the world are no longer relevant. They are forced to learn new behaviours, understand new rules and to adapt to new values and another type of social organisation. Becoming a refugee is therefore a source of deep learning as they confront unexpected changes in their life plans and the need to reshape their lives and reconstruct their identities. This study and the narratives are about the processes of learning and identity formation which accompany the struggle of forced migrants to establish themselves in a new context.

The book, and the research on which it is based, is located in a particular historical moment. The last two decades have witnessed dramatic increases in the movement of people around the globe, both labour migration and refugees. The UK and other wealthy countries in the global north have become the recipients of increasing numbers of migrants, and controlling national borders has become a major preoccupation. The issue of asylum has been the subject of particularly intense political and public debate; it is rarely out of the media spotlight, with reporting often being hostile and unbalanced. Much of the attention focuses around the numbers entering the UK, and concern that too many refugees are coming, attracted by generous welfare benefits.

The first decade of the twenty first century has seen major terrorist attacks in Western cities and an ensuing 'war on terror'. This has given added momentum to ongoing debates and concerns around citizenship, social cohesion and multiculturalism. It has also added to the negative associations around refugees and asylum seekers, who are increasingly represented as threatening national identity and security. Refugees are not only seen as a 'burden' on an overstretched welfare system, but as a security threat, and as a feared 'other', threatening national identity and social cohesion (Castles, 2003; Lynn and Lea, 2003; Bloch and Schuster, 2005; Yuval-Davis *et al*, 2005). This fear is reflected in the growing racist intolerance shown against migrants and refugees across Europe (Zetter, 2007), and the increasingly assimilationist approaches to social integration. It is within this historical context that public perception, social discourses and policy responses to refugees are being determined, and which in turn shape and construct the experiences of those seeking asylum in the UK and their subjectivities.

We know that the UK is home to a significant number of refugees who are highly qualified and have professional backgrounds. For example, a skills audit of refugees published by the Home Office (Kirk, 2004) found that 32 per cent of men and 25 per cent of women had undergraduate or postgraduate qualifications and 37 per cent were in professional or managerial occupations before coming to the UK. Despite these high levels of human capital, unemployment and under-employment among refugees remains high. The Department for Work and Pensions (DWP) estimate that the national average for unemployment of refugees is around 36 per cent (Bloch, 2002). Where refugees are working in the UK it is often far below their capabilities. Many highly qualified professionals work in unskilled casual jobs, unrelated to their qualifications or past professional experience (Dumper, 2002; Jonker, 2004).

The focus of this book is on refugees who arrive in the UK with high level professional qualifications. One feature they all share is their professional and social class background; this has formed one of the main sources of their identity formation. All had enjoyed class privilege and, in some cases, gender privilege in their country of origin. They had been accustomed to the respect and respectability associated with high status employment and social position, and one of the universal concerns of all participants was an attempt to re-establish their respectability and professional identity. The stories of refugees from the poorest strata of society are missing from this study.

Theoretical and conceptual framework

> ... know that many personal troubles cannot be solved merely as troubles, but must be understood in terms of public issues ... Know that the problems of social science, when adequately formulated, must include both troubles and issues, both biography and history, and the range of their intricate relations. Within that range the life of the individual and the making of society occur; and that within that range the sociological imagination has its chance to make a difference in the quality of human life in our times. (Wright Mills, 1959:226)

The individual lives and experiences of refugees cannot be understood without reference to wider social conditions, or what Wright Mills refers to as 'public issues'. He highlights the value of personal narrative as a source of knowledge and understanding of the world, and stresses the interplay between the personal and social levels, the self and the world, biography and history. Neither the individual nor the social world can be understood without understanding both, and the task of the sociological imagination is to range from the most intimate features of human lives to the most remote and abstract. This section sets out the theoretical and conceptual understandings which underpin this research and help us understand these 'personal troubles'.

Habitus, capital and field

In order to try and capture this complex interplay between structure and agency, between subjective experience and objective conditions, I have drawn on the work of Pierre Bourdieu (1977; 1998; 1999). Bourdieu's framework of habitus, capital and field provide useful explanatory tools for apprehending the relationship between the social world and the individual, and for understanding the movement through social space which occurs with migration. They enable us to conceptualise the individual and the social as being in a dialectical relationship so that social structures and cultures impinge on individual agency and are in turn reproduced through the social action of individuals.

Bourdieu describes habitus as a system of durable, embodied dispositions, expressed through ways of speaking, gesturing, standing, thinking and feeling. They derive from our social background and upbringing so that according to Bourdieu not only is the body in the social world, but the social world is also in the body (Bourdieu, 1977 and 1998). When we are in a social world, or field, of which we are a product, we do not feel or notice the tacit rules, norms and traditions which govern activity. Instead we experience them in a taken for granted or unthinking way.

Connected to habitus are the various forms of capital – cultural, social, symbolic and economic – which individuals can draw upon to secure advantage in particular fields. Cultural capital can exist in 'incorporated' or embodied states, 'ie. in the form of long-lasting dispositions of the mind and body' (2004:17), which are an integral part of the person. Examples of embodied cultural capital include language skills, aspirations, having the right accent, being familiar with particular academic discourses. Cultural capital also exists in institutionalised states, for example in the form of academic qualifications, which confer institutional recognition on the individual. Refugees in the UK can be rich in both of these forms of cultural capital; they may come with high levels of institutional cultural capital in the form of academic and professional qualifications. Many speak several languages and have well developed communication skills attained through their multi-lingual experiences. They have often come from backgrounds where education and academic achievement are highly regarded, and they have high aspirations for themselves and their children. They have an array of cultural and professional knowledge and understanding gained from their previous lives.

Social capital consists of the social ties and networks which can function as a resource and bring advantage to those who possess them (Bourdieu and Wacquant, 1992; Bourdieu, 2004). Generally, discussions of social capital follow Putnam (2004) and make the distinction between 'bonding' and 'bridging' social capital. Bonding social capital consists of the close ties we have with people who are similar to us, for example friends, family, neighbours; this form of social capital is useful for 'getting by'. Bridging social capital is composed of the looser networks which link us with more distant acquaintances from other social groups and circles. This latter social capital is essential for 'getting on' as it links us into resources, ideas and information outside of our own social milieu and can provide the know-how to achieve goals and bring advantage (Putnam, 2000; Field, 2005). I have argued elsewhere that while refugee communities may be rich in bonding social capital, they tend to be excluded from the bridging social capital and the learning within them (Morrice, 2007).

In order for the different capitals to be used and to bring advantage to their possessor, they have to be in a social world or field where they are perceived and recognised as legitimate. Only when they have been recognised can the different capitals be converted into symbolic capital, which brings with it symbolic power. The conversion of capital into symbolic capital is a collective undertaking and 'cannot succeed without the complicity of the whole group: the work of denial which is the source of social alchemy is, like magic, a collective undertaking' (Bourdieu, 1977:195). The collective denial, or misrecognition, of the arbitrary nature of whatever symbolic capital is at stake, masks the vested interests of the most powerful in maintaining relations of inequality. Direct violence or overt discrimination can be dispensed with, the subordinate positioning of marginalised groups such as refugees is reproduced through structures of perception and appreciation which are presented as natural. The inferior positioning of refugees becomes obscured and instead distinction is legitimated under the guise of individual ability or virtue. Linguistic, cultural, ethnic and other forms of symbolic dominance are presented as natural, and their social origins – the fact that they are the product of the objective structure of society – remain hidden and go unrecognised. In this way inequalities and systematic disempowerment are engendered. The correspondence between the objective order and the subjective principles of organisation, the natural and the social world, appear as self-evident (Bourdieu, 1977:164). Bourdieu describes this consent of both dominating and dominated as constituting symbolic violence, 'the gentle, invisible form of violence, which is never recognised as such...' (1977:192).

Bourdieu argues that habitus and field work together and inform each other; they need to be conceptualised and analysed in tandem. To fully comprehend individual agency and the phenomenologies of individuals, these have to be located within an analysis of field. For refugees, an analysis of field includes an understanding of the extent to which refugees' social and cultural capital is valued and can be converted to bring economic or educational reward. An individual's ability to draw upon these resources and, crucially, to have them recognised as valuable, significantly impacts on the way in which they respond to and cope with migration and conditions in the UK. An analysis of field also includes an understanding of how policy and social discourses construct the category of refugee, and assign particular social roles and identities while denying others; and how these institutionalised mechanisms construct and curtail opportunities for the conversion and transformation of capitals.

For the refugees in this book, the habitus that they were born into, and the cultural and social capital acquired, enabled them to move quite smoothly through education and into professional positions in their country. Their capitals and habitus existed in a field in which it was recognised and could be employed. However, migration involves movement to a new social space where the capital accumulated might not be recognised as legitimate and may not have exchange value. Similarly, habitus operates at an unconscious level until it encounters a new field of which it is not a product. At this point it becomes:

> ... a habitus divided against itself, in constant negotiation with itself and its ambivalence, and therefore doomed to a kind of duplication, to a double perception of self, to successive allegiances and multiple identities. (1999: 511)

At these moments of non-continuity the embodied dispositions, expressed through ways of speaking, gesturing, standing, thinking and feeling, are no longer experienced in an unthinking or taken for granted way. Such times of dislocation from the past suggest periods of disorientation, great uncertainty, and a questioning of self. They also generate periods of intense reflection and learning.

Biographical learning

In educational research there has been growing interest in understanding learning processes and experiences from the perspective of the learner. Such methodological approaches aim to elucidate experiences and dispositions to learning across the lifespan. The terms learning career, learning lifecycle, educational biography, life history, auto/biography, life narrative, learning lives and learning identity have all been used to describe the process. Each term reveals a different approach and focus (Bertaux, 1981; Dominice, 2000). In much of this research the concepts of learning, biography, agency and identity are closely linked.

All of the approaches have in common an interest in the subjective reality of the individual, how they interpret, understand and define their social world. The advantage of adapting a biographical or life history approach, as Armstrong (1987) has pointed out, is that unlike most social and educational research which fragments aspects of people's lives, by for example focusing only on formal education, or by divorcing the study from social or cultural factors, it enables us to focus on the totality of an individual's life. It enables us to relate individual lives and social events to social contexts, to explore how personal experiences are woven into the social fabric. In order to understand an individual's life we need to take account of their inheritance from the past; the cultural, social and economic structures in which they grew up. There is also the assumption that an individual's biography is sequential, and that no one point can be understood without looking at what preceded it. The approach also enables us to see individuals with a future, with hopes and fears and dreams.

Alheit and Dausien (2002) put forward the idea of the 'biographicity' of social learning processes, by which they mean 'theoretical perspective on education and training that takes as its starting point the life history perspective of the actual learner' (2002:11). It recognises the capacity of individuals to compose a biography and develop reflexivity. A skill which social theorists such as Giddens (1991) and Beck (1992) consider to be essential in a perpetually changing, individualised social world, where biographical trajectories are less certain. It is a world in which 'the self becomes a reflexive project' (Giddens, 1991:32).

Throughout the life course we acquire ways of understanding and knowing the world around us. These consist not only of experience and dispositions but also the systems for appropriating the social world. Much of this knowledge is pre-reflexive and is acquired implicitly or tacitly, it is taken for granted so that

> ... we 'move' within our biographically acquired landscape of knowledge, without consciously reflecting on every step we take ... In many cases, we do not turn to such elements in our biographical 'background knowledge' until we find ourselves stumbling, or at a crossroads ... (Alheit and Dausien, 2002: 15)

This sense of 'stumbling', or of being 'at a crossroads', clearly resonates with Bourdieu's notion of a disjuncture between field and habitus. These critical moments of learning in an individual's life have been widely recognised by educationalists. For example, Jarvis (2006) refers to episodes when there is '[a] feeling of disharmony with the life-world'. He goes on to suggest that the need to try and re-establish harmony 'may be amongst the most important motivating factors for most individuals to learn (2006a:78 and 77). Similarly, Mezirow's (1990 and 2000) work on transformative learning is based on the proposition that when an individual's 'frame of reference' is discordant with their experience a 'disorientating dilemma occurs' and that through critical reflection and learning they transform their perspective.

For Alheit and Dausien, life itself is a field of learning. They have developed the notion of biographical learning, which is:

> ... a self-willed, 'autopoetic' accomplishment on the part of active subjects in which they reflectively 'organise' their experience in such a way that they also generate personal coherence, identity, a meaning to their life history and a communicable, socially viable life world perspective for guiding their actions (Alheit, 2005:209).

Biographical or life course approaches to learning can be seen as an attempt to transcend the dichotomy between the wider social forces which shape and interact with individual lives and the issue of individual agency and the way individual responses and actions can vary considerably from person to person (West *et al*, 2007). It is an approach which offers not only the subjective perspective of refugees but also a temporal dimension to understanding learning processes and identity formation. Drawing on life history, it recognises the skills, education, jobs, culture, identity and social roles which refugees occupied prior to migration, and how these pre-migration characteristics influence and shape learning processes and identity construction in a new context. Biographical research is particularly suited to exploring how people actively learn their world and their place within it. It enables us to capture changes in how individuals conceptualise their present, but also how their past is interpreted in new and often conflicting ways in the light of present circumstances (Merrill and West, 2009).

Understanding identity

The concept of identity occupies a prominent place in contemporary social science research and has been subject to much scholarly debate and critique. Different academic and intellectual discourses draw on different understandings and different uses of the concept. Hall (1992) provides a useful sketch of the philosophical assumptions underlying different conceptualisations. He suggests that three models of identity are associate with modernity: the Enlightenment subject, the sociological subject, and the post-modern subject. The first of these conceptualises the subject as being a unified individual, with an inner core which unfolds as the individual grows and develops, but which remains essentially the same throughout the individual's life. The second model, the sociological subject, emerges from the growing complexity of the modern world and places greater emphasis on the interactive nature of identity. Here, identity mediates the individual's active exchange with their social environment, as well as the internalisation of socially significant meanings and values. Hall emphasises that this conception of identity still assumes an inner core, but it is one which is 'formed and modified in a continuous dialogue with the cultural worlds 'outside' and the identities which they offer' (1992:276). The third and final conceptualisation, the post-modern subject, is a product of the structural and cultural changes of late modernity. This subject has no single essential identity which serves as a stable core at the centre of the individual. Instead identities are permanently shifting; they are the product of specific historical, cultural and institutional sites within specific discursive formations.

> ... identities are never unified and, in late modern times, increasingly fragmented and fractured; never singular but multiply constructed across different, often intersecting and antagonistic, discourses, practices and positions. (Hall, 2000:17)

I have adopted a post-structuralist approach to identity, which recognises that the self is an ongoing project in which human subjects are in a continual process of 'becoming'. As human subjects we are always circumscribed by particular situations and the discourses at work. These both constitute subjectivities in particular ways and position individuals within particular discourses. The duality of this process whereby individuals are both subjected and become agentic subjects in the process is described by Davies:

> The subject is both dominated and shaped and, at the same time and through the same practices, actively takes up the possibilities of the self that are available in recognised/recognisable discourses and practices. (Davies, 2006:79)

In terms of subjective construction and availability of social positions, the process of migration to a new social space is double edged. To varying degrees, migration severs the subject from the social practices, discourses and structures of the culture in which they had grown up, and through which their habitus had enabled them to move in a fairly smooth and perhaps largely unreflective way. Movement to a new social space opens up possibilities for reflection on the discourses through which the self has been constituted. It creates opportunities for change and possibilities for exploring and taking up new subject positions, for deconstructing and reconstructing identities. The predictable and culturally familiar identities associated with, for example class, gender, ethnicity and sexuality are no longer certain in the new social space, and the self is exposed to new and alternative discursive practices.

In particular, migration offers a loosening of traditional gender identities and the inherited ascriptions associated with gender, enabling a different kind of gender performance and practice. On the other hand, however, the new social space has its own discourses, subject positions and scripts. Which social positions are available and which are denied is central to subject formation and to this study. Essentialised social scripts and positions, which have to be managed and negotiated, are imposed upon refugees. While wider discourses shape the identity strategies available, each individual will respond differently, in biographically informed ways. Understanding identity through the narratives which individuals tell, chronicles the way identity is constantly changing in response to events and experiences in the life history and also how the way that these experiences are represented constitute their current way of being.

Underpinned by these theoretical and conceptual understandings, this book sets out to understand how refugees negotiate and manage the transition to living in the UK. In particular it is concerned to explore how individual biography shapes and informs the strategies adopted by refugees in the UK and what insight learning (both informal and formal) can offer to our understanding of the processes involved in transition to the UK. Before moving on to the individual narratives a note about the methodological and ethical considerations is needed.

A note on methodology

The rebuilding of fractured lives is a long and complex process, particularly as refugees in the UK face multiple exclusionary processes. In order to capture the temporal nature of transition, I adopted a longitudinal approach: interviewing a group of twelve refugees over a period of five years (2004-2009). Participants for the research were identified from their participation in a University of Sussex course called *Ways into Learning and Work* (WILAW). The course was specifically designed and developed to support refugees with higher level and professional qualifications to access either HE or employment (Morrice, 2005).

To allow sufficient space and depth for each story, only five have been presented here. I have chosen two men, both from Iran, and three women, from Iraq, Iran and Zimbabwe. The stories have been selected for the way they highlight different facets of refugee experiences. Each provides a different insight, whether experience as a parent, being single and alone, the experience of the asylum system itself, the type of educational capital possessed and so on. All point to the varied facets and challenges of being a refugee.

In adopting a longitudinal approach, I aimed to provide a more holistic understanding of the transition process, one which can incorporate the interplay of diverse factors over time and illuminate how the experience of living in the UK changes over time. The process of transition is long and on-going; it often involves constant adjustments and readjustments in response to changing circumstances and situations. The longitudinal method recognises the temporal unfolding of opportunities, of setbacks and revisions to life plans and changes in aspirations. The temporal aspect provides opportunity to identify coherence and consistency in narratives, and at the same time can capture moments when the cohesive narrative presentations and theorisations of self might become disrupted or challenged. Plumridge and Thomson (2003) suggest that longitudinal studies foreground the 'subject in process' and the 'provisionality of identity work'. As a method then, it would appear to be particularly relevant to the process of migration where change continues over a period of time.

There are inevitable limitations to the narrative mode of enquiry. By asking participants to reflect back and recall events and activities which took place in the past, we are creating what Hammerton and Thomson (2005) call 'memory stories'. That is, stories told from, and possibly reinterpreted by, the present life circumstances and identity of the narrator. Issues of what a narrator chooses to recall and relate, and the reliability of memory, are pertinent to narrative enquiry and need to be subject to scrutiny and questioning throughout the research process (Hammerton and Thomson, 2005).

The stories presented here have been selected and constructed in a complex and multi-layered process. The process starts with the individual, what they choose to remember and how they choose to story themselves. Interviews themselves are 'inherently social encounters' in which 'interviewees and interviewers work to construct themselves as certain types of people in relation to the topic of the interview and reflexively the interview itself' (Rapley, 2001:303). So the stories are re-told and co-constructed with me, a white, female academic – they are social constructs, products of a particular moment and encounter. Finally I have reinterpreted and repackaged the stories for this research and this book. As Merrill and West (2009) highlight, the term 'auto/biographical' research is often used to draw attention to the inter-relationship between the biography of the researcher and the researched:

> ... those constructions we make of others in writing their life histories contain and reflect our own histories and social and cultural locations as well as psychologies. (Merrill and West, 2009)

Cross-cultural research requires particular sensitivity and reflexivity. I have tried to remain mindful of my own cultural expectations and frames of reference in creating and constructing these narratives.

I viewed the interview process as an interactive and fluid process, rather than a process of merely eliciting information and listening. I engaged in discussion, sometimes offering personal information about myself and my family, or responding to requests for advice or opinion. Over the research period my relationship with participants developed from the boundaried research relationship of researcher and participant and spilled over into friendship. The research became a more personal, reciprocal and dialogical process. Between formal interviews I met up with participants socially for a cup of tea or coffee; sometimes these meetings were prompted by a request to sign a passport or citizenship application, or to look over a job application or CV. At other times, they were simply to have a chat and catch up on recent events, or to celebrate achievement, for example at university graduation ceremonies.

It is never possible to divorce oneself completely from one's research interests and the spilling over of the research process into more personal territory raises particular ethical issues. The informality increases the possibility of 'unthinking disclosure', particularly around more personal issues, such as relationships or mental health. I was acutely aware that what was told to me during these informal meetings could not be used as part of my research. When information relevant to my research questions emerged, I asked directly whether they would be willing to recount the story when we next met for a taped interview. In most instances participants were willing to retell the story; where they weren't their privacy and integrity has been respected and none of the information, or exchange has been used.

Ethical considerations and research with refugees

Working with refugees raises particular ethical issues. In considering the ethical issues around research I have been particularly guided by Plummer's work in life history (Plummer, 2001). Refugees are likely to have experienced interviewing, questioning and possible interrogation both in the country they have fled from, and on arrival in the UK. On arrival in the UK they have had to present and 'story' their experiences for Home Office officials, who have then judged whether the story is credible and whether it fits within their guidelines for granting refugee status. Particular sensitivity and reflexivity is required to ensure that participants are clear about the purposes and possible uses of the research. Previous research with refugees has drawn attention to the need to ensure that participation in research does not cause harm to their current situation or to their family remaining in the country of origin (Yu and Liu, 1986; Jacobsen and Landau, 2003).

Issues of confidentiality, anonymity and consent were explained to all my participants, both at the point of inviting them to participate in the research and at the start of the first interview. All were asked to sign a conditions of use and consent form. From the outset I have been guided by the ethical principles of attempting to avoid potential negative consequences for participants, or for the broader refugee community. However, ethical considerations are complex, on-going and dynamic so require constant re-thinking and re-negotiation. Thomson (2003) talks of a 'parallelogram of ethical responsibilities'; each corner of the parallelogram represents a different responsibility: to the narrator, to significant others, to history (and research) and to the researcher. The corners are often in tension and require constant negotiation. I have found this a useful metaphor for conceptualising and thinking through some of the ethical dilemmas and tensions raised during this research. In the significant others corner I include responsibilities to the refugee community, so how do you handle narratives that reproduce negative stereotypes around refugees and asylum seekers, for example? Or the narrative which tells of issues which in their own community might be considered taboo, for example issues of sexuality? Researchers have a duty to be mindful of the context in which research is produced.

The participants in the research were all asked to select a pseudonym. However, working in a city which has a relatively small refugee community, and working with an even smaller sub-set of that community, it is difficult to guarantee complete anonymity only with pseudonyms. While I have tried to change or 'blur' possible identifying elements in their stories, I have also chosen to omit some aspects of some stories to avoid causing potential harm or distress to participants or their families. Similarly, I have taken particular care to ensure that my research cannot be used to reproduce or contribute to the negative discourses around refugees and asylum seekers.

To understand the strategies that refugees adopt in the UK and why they negotiate their new environment in the way they do, it is necessary to understand their past. Refugees in this study have experienced degrees of fear, persecution, loss, separation and trauma that is unimaginable to most of us. For this reason I avoided a traditional life history approach of asking participants to recount their life story at the first interview. Rather, the initial interviews were 'real time' interviews and concerned life and experiences in the UK; only once I felt a level of trust had been established did we move to the in-depth interviews about life before they came to the UK. In reality of course, many of the interviews did not fall neatly into either only being about the past, or only being in real time. Instead, most involved some interweaving of past stories and memories with the present, but in the initial interviews this was participant initiated and led.

I was also aware that there are aspects of the refugee story which are likely to be particularly sensitive, upsetting or traumatic; these include details of their reason for fleeing their country, their experiences immediately prior to flight, and their journey to the UK. I decided not to ask them directly about these issues, but instead left it up to the refugees themselves to decide how much they told me. Some were quite willing to talk about their experiences of persecution and flight; others have never revealed this part of their narrative or have only hinted at aspects of it. One participant talked about their experiences, but requested that this part of their story not be included in this research.

Unlike much other life history work, my questions focused on the practical aspects of their stories rather than the emotional aspects. In part this was because my research questions were primarily concerned with the practical aspects of the transition process, and in part it was to try and avoid putting participants in a position where they were asked to explore and relive potentially painful experiences.

As Plummer (2001) reminds us, there is always an asymmetrical power relation between researcher and researched, and by asking about people's lives we might be asking them to speak of 'traumas hitherto unnamed' and in so doing 'to solidify and consolidate in words a kind of life. And for this ... the researcher becomes responsible' (Plummer, 2001:225). Although not explicitly addressed in the research, the emotional distress generated by the doubts and insecurities of living and being a refugee are present in the narratives in varying degrees.

These ethical considerations inevitably mean that there are silences and gaps in the narratives presented. Despite some issues being 'the elephant in the room' during the research process, these are areas I have chosen either not to probe or not to write about. The silences are apparent and important in the narratives and should be read as just that: what is present but not spoken.

The structure of the book

Chapter two considers contemporary migration and draws attention to some of the complexities and debates surrounding the international movement of people. Increases in population movements around the globe have led to a shift in UK (and European) immigration policy, and taken discourses around asylum issues in a particular direction. This policy context and the widespread hostility and suspicion towards refugees will be examined. Chapter three identifies some key perspectives on learning which frame and inform the experiences and identity processes associated with becoming a refugee. The rise of the concept of lifelong learning is examined, and how contemporary conceptions of learning afford greater attention and recognition to informal and non-formal learning in people's lives.

The heart of this book is the narratives of five refugees and these are set out in chapters four to eight. They illustrate how each refugee has his or her own personal story which is individual to them and linked to their unique biographical, cultural and social background. Each of these chapters falls into two parts: life prior to migration and life in the UK. However, they vary in the space devoted to each part of the story, and which aspects of the migration and transition process are fore grounded.

The narratives presented illuminate the hybridity of experience and indicate how the migration process itself frames responses and adaptations to life in the UK. Each narrative is lived within the broader social script of what it means to be a refugee in the UK, and how this script is negotiated, managed and sometimes subverted in different ways. These experiences cross cut and intersect with differences of ethnicity, of gender, of country of origin, faith and age.

In chapters nine and ten I draw out the common themes in these narratives. Chapter nine considers how refugees' experiences and subjectivities are constructed and shaped by broader social structures and practices. These symbolic systems impose identities and curtail the position-taking available to refugees. It explores the strategies adopted and the dynamic interplay between externally imposed narratives and the identities harboured by refugees themselves. Unable to articulate being a refugee as a positive identity, the participants draw on alternative discourses so as to present themselves as having moral worth and respectability.

Chapter ten considers more explicitly the learning processes at work in the transition to life in the UK. I suggest there is a subterranean, hidden curriculum of beliefs, norms and expectations which are largely accessed through informal and non-formal learning. In seeking to understand the depth and complexity of subjective construction and identity formation, I suggest conceptualising learning as processes of 'becoming' and 'unbecoming' (Biesta, 2006; Hodkinson *et al*, 2007) has greater purchase. Lastly, I consider how participants use higher education as a route to re-establishing a professional identity and career in the UK, and also to construct a morally acceptable identity for themselves.

The final chapter draws together the strands running through the book and suggests some of the patterns and differences in the experiences of refugees and what we can claim to know about the lives of refugees in the UK today. The discussion revisits some of the recent debates in lifelong learning and re-examines the policy context around asylum seekers and refugees. Some of the most problematic areas of policy are discussed in the light of what has been learned from the case studies. The implications of policy, both intended and unintended, on the lives of refugees are highlighted and the book ends with reflection on what practitioners might be able to draw from this study.

2

The changing context of migration and the UK Government's policy response

Contemporary migration

Castles and Miller (2003) identify five general trends in contemporary migration which are worth paraphrasing here. *Globalisation*: a tendency for more countries to be affected by migration and a broader spectrum of economic, social and cultural background of migrants. The *acceleration* of migration: the quantitative growth in population movements in all major regions; the *differentiation* of migration: countries are experiencing a range of types of migration at once, eg. labour migration and refugees. The *feminisation* of migration: women play a significant role in all regions and in most, but not all, types of migration. Finally, the growing *politicisation* of migration: national and international security policies and domestic politics are increasingly affected by international migration.

Alongside the increased movement of people, the study of migration has increased dramatically. The field has been dominated by geography, sociology and economics with growing contributions from other disciplines such as psychology, anthropology, history and political science. Each of the disciplines has its own methods, theories and research foci, although approaches overlap and build upon each other. Early theories of migration focused on the individual, who was conceptualised as a rational being weighing up the costs and benefits to themselves and their families of moving. The causes of migration were perceived to lie in a combination of 'push factors', compelling people to leave a particular country, and 'pull factors' attracting them to certain other countries. These individualistic theories have been criticised for being ahistorical, for ignoring the structural inequalities between rich and poor nations and the constraints these impose on choices and decision-making.

From the 1970s an alternative approach to migration was provided which stressed the unequal distribution of economic and political power in the world economy. The historical-structural approach had its roots in Marxist political economy and world systems theory. These theorists argue that migration perpetuated uneven development by exploiting the resources of poor countries (cheap labour) to make the rich even richer (see eg. Castles and Kosack, 1973). Migration could not be understood as individuals exercising free choice, because structural inequalities had drained resources from poor countries, compelling individuals to migrate. The historical-structuralist account has been criticised for overplaying the interests of capital and reducing migrants to passive pawns of international capitalism (Kofman *et al*, 2000). It was also argued that divisions of gender and non-economic causes of migration tended to be overlooked (Sales, 2007).

A new approach to migration, migration systems theory, emerged from these critiques of individualistic and historical-structural accounts of migration. This approach attempts to cover all dimensions of the migration experience by proposing a three-tier conception of migration, encompassing micro-, meso- and macro-structures. It is based on the principle that migratory movements can be understood as a result of the interaction between them (Castles and Miller, 2003; Sales, 2007).

The macro-level includes the migration system or regime governing relations between receiving and sending countries: the laws, structures and practices established by those states, eg. governing entry requirements and the rights of migrants. It also includes the political economy of the world market. The meso-level provides a link between the two. It includes the individuals, groups and organisations which take a mediating role between migrants, and political and economic institutions. These include lawyers, recruitment organisations, agents and people traffickers (Harris, 1996 cited in Castles and Miller, 2003).

The micro-structures focus on the individual migrant's experience, their history, resources and the social identities which shape their migratory strategy. It includes the informal social networks and social capital developed by migrants to manage the migration process, and this has become an increasingly important focus for migration research (Portes, 2004). The micro-level recognises migrants as social beings with particular attributes: gender, social class, ethnicity, religion, age and stage in the life cycle. These social differences cross-cut and interact effecting migratory strategies, life chances and the cultural, economic, social and political resources which can be drawn upon in the new social space which migrants find themselves. It also creates space for an understanding of human agency and how migration is experienced and managed differently by different social actors.

Refugees

The boundaries between those who are considered to be 'voluntary' migrants, eg. labour migrants, family reunification etc., and those who are considered 'forced' migrants, who flee wars, natural disasters etc., are contentious and not clear cut. Only a small proportion of migrants are considered to be forced migrants, and those who are able to claim refugee status are an even smaller group. In 2010 the United Nations (UN) estimated that just 7.6 per cent of all international migrants were refugees. This represents a reduction from 8.8 per cent in 2000 and 11.9 per cent in 1990 (UN, 2009).

The formal definition of a refugee, set out in the UN Convention Relating to the Status of Refugees 1951, is based on individuals fleeing persecution and is the basis for international refugee law. It defines a refugee as a person who

> ... owing to well-founded fear of being persecuted for reasons of race, religion, nationality, membership of a particular social group, or political opinion, is outside the country of his nationality, and is unable to or, owing to such fear, is unwilling to avail himself of the protection of that country...
> (Article 1 A(2) cited in UNHCR, 2007a)

Originally drawn up to protect the millions of internationally displaced Europeans after the Second World War, the scope was expanded in 1967 to cover all refugees. The legal definition of a refugee is used in contrast to asylum seeker, which refers to a person who has applied for asylum, but whose application has not yet been concluded.

The definition of a refugee has been increasingly criticised on a number of grounds. It focuses on an individual's right to claim asylum rather than a concept of claiming asylum on a collective basis; it largely ignores gendered forms of persecution and is very narrow (Sales, 2007). The growing impact of climate change on the sustainability of life in parts of the world, and the uneven outcomes of globalisation processes, have meant that the reasons for migration have inevitably become increasingly complex. Poverty, environmental degradation, human rights abuses, poor governance converge in a far more complicated way than anything imagined half a century ago when the UN Convention was drawn up. This has led some commentators to argue that the legal definition is no longer able to capture the more complex forms of persecution and human rights abuses linked to economic failure, the breakdown of state structures and the associated rise of political cliques and dictatorships. To try and capture more tangled forms of persecution and the links between refugee movements and international migration more generally, 'forced migrant' has increasingly been used in research literature. However, this dilutes the notion of refugees as a distinct category of people in need of international protection and could lead to states watering down their commitments to refugees. The United Nations High Commissioner for Refugees (UNHCR) in particular has resisted attempts to broaden the refugee notion to encompass groups other than those fleeing on grounds of persecution. It points to the uniqueness of the legal status of refugees under international law, and the importance of maintaining a clear distinction between refugees and migrants in public and political opinion (UNHCR, 2007b).

Globalisation and in particular electronic communication mean that the refugee diasporas are no longer atomised and disconnected either from 'home' or from co-ethnics and co-nationals in their place of origin (Castles, 2003; Zetter, 2007). This gives rise to what Zetter calls a 'here and there belonging' of refugees where belonging/home are complex notions decoupled from locality and physical entity. He describes the way in which refugees manage multiple identities:

> ... belonging to but also excluded from their host society and, because they are refugees, belonging to but also excluded from their country/society of origin. Simultaneously cohering to different social worlds and communities ... (Zetter, 2007:187).

The notion of a nation state as the focus of social belonging is further complicated when we consider that many refugees have family members and loved ones in exile in other countries, giving rise to a range of social, economic, political and other ties connecting co-nationals across the globe. It is clear that belonging is complex, and has a number of dimensions which are about more than affiliation to a nation state and the rights and duties entailed in this. Belonging has an important affective dimension and includes how and whether people feel that they are included, and the extent to which they can participate in a society or community. A sense of belonging is therefore generated as much through feeling excluded or included, as a formal entitlement to live and remain in a particular country.

UK context and government policy response

From the late 1980s through to the summer of 2003 the UK witnessed a dramatic increase in the number of people applying for asylum and went from being a marginal recipient of asylum seekers to one of the most significant in the European Union (Griffiths *et al*, 2005). However, since 2003 asylum applications have declined year on year. Recent figures indicate that there were 24,485 applications in 2009 (Home Office, 2009a) compared with a peak of 84,130 applications in 2002. There has been a similar decline in applications to other states who were members of the European Union before 1 April 2004. Over the last decade the top applicant nationalities to the UK have been Iraq, Afghanistan, Somalia, Zimbabwe, Iran and China (Home Office, 2009a).

In the light of the intensity of public debate around asylum issues and the concerns that the UK is being 'swamped' by asylum applicants, it is worth remembering that the majority of refugees still remain in the global south. The UNHCR estimated that in 2009 80 per cent of the world's refugees were being looked after in developing countries, with Pakistan, Iran and Syria hosting the largest numbers. Just 16 per cent were being looked after in Europe, with the UK offering protection to just 3 per cent of the world's refugees (UNHCR, 2010). The small minority who do claim asylum in the UK or Europe tend to be those with greater economic resources, social and human capital, especially education.

In a review of immigration policy in the UK since 1997, Flynn (2005) describes the shift in UK government policy from a 'Fortress Britain' vision of the 70s and 80s which aimed to severely restrict numbers coming to the UK, to policies of managed migration of the New Labour government. He argues that this shift has come about through recognition of the need for higher levels of migration to sustain modern developed economies, and as a result migration policy has been reconfigured around economic interests. It is businesses and employers who decide which skill groups can enter the UK and what rights they are entitled to. A points-based system of immigration has been introduced to ensure that migrants gaining access to the UK have the skills the economy needs (Somerville, 2007; Sales, 2007).

Alongside recognition of the economic value of migration the government has developed a more restrictive approach to asylum seekers and has attempted to harden the distinction between asylum seekers and refugees. Those who arrive at the UK's borders seeking refugee status evoke fears of loss of state control (Flynn, 2005; Castles, 2003). They have been subject to increasingly restrictive legislation to control their spontaneous or 'unmanaged' movement. Yuval Davis *et al* (2005) make the point that while the UK government recognises that migration is an inevitable reality of the modern and globalised world, and one which enables it to cherry pick the most skilled and educated workforce from Third World countries, it has to balance these benefits with perceived domestic tensions around social integration and community cohesion.

Since 1999 the UK Government has introduced five migration related Acts of Parliament. These are: *The Immigration and Asylum Act* (Home Office, 1999), *The Nationality, Immigration and Asylum Act* (Home Office, 2002), *The Asylum and Immigration (Treatment of Claimants, etc.)* Act (Home Office, 2004), *The Immigration, Asylum, and Nationality Act (IAN)* (Home Office, 2006), and *The Borders, Citizenship and Immigration Act 2009* (Home Office, 2009). The major theme running through the legislation has been a tightening of immigration controls and the swifter removal of unsuccessful asylum applicants. A clear distinction is made between asylum seekers, who have generally been portrayed as being more numerous and 'undeserving', and 'genuine' refugees who need a 'fairer' system.

The 1999 Act introduced the policy of dispersal which removed asylum applicants from the benefit system and created the National Asylum Support Service (NASS) to support and disperse destitute asylum seekers around the country. The Government policy of dispersal was driven by the wish to avoid refugees being concentrated in a few places, such as London, where they might be perceived as putting pressure on housing stock, community resources and the labour market. It can also be seen as a more general process of European Union harmonisation of reception policies (Griffiths *et al*, 2005). However, it denies newly arrived asylum seekers the opportunity to continue the migration chain and settle with family and friends already in the UK. Robinson (2003) argues the concept of dispersal is based upon two premises; the first is that the arrival of refugees is a national 'problem', the burden of which should be shared. The second is that:

> The right of the indigenous population to live in communities where their cultures and identities are not challenged by the non-conforming groups should be privileged over the rights of refugees. Refugees, then, are consequently denied the opportunity to congregate in clustered ethnic communities, with all the benefits these provide new and old arrivals alike. (2003: 23)

Other measures have excluded asylum seekers from welfare services such as social housing and non-emergency healthcare, reduced asylum appeal rights and increased the detention estate (Bloch and Schuster, 2005). In July 2002 asylum seekers were prevented from working and excluded from the labour market. The main asylum applicant (usually male) can apply for permission to work if they have waited more than twelve months for an initial decision by the Home Office.

From September 2010 the immigration rules were amended so that asylum seekers who fall within this category are restricted to national shortage occupations (Refugee Council, 2010a). From 2007 asylum seekers were also excluded from access to ESOL and other publicly funded Further Education courses (LSC, 2006). However, following a Race Equality Impact Assessment, eligibility was reinstated for Further Education (excluding work-based training) for those asylum seekers whose asylum claim has taken more than six months to settle or who have been refused asylum in the UK but who are unable to leave the UK due to circumstances beyond their control (ie. Those who are eligible for support under Section 4 of the Immigration and Asylum Act 1999) (DfES, 2007).

In November 2010 the new Conservative led Coalition Government outlined its plans for ESOL provision in the strategy document *Further Education – New Horizon.* From 2011/2012 there will be an overall reduction in ESOL funding per student, and publicly funded ESOL provision will be restricted to people who are on 'active benefits' such as Job Seekers Allowance and Employment Support Allowance. Refugees who are on income support, for example carers, parents and the elderly will not be eligible for funding. Under current proposals funding will be unavailable to the spouses and partners of those on 'active benefit'; this will particularly affect women wishing to learn English. Funding for ESOL delivered in the workplace will also be cut (BIS, 2010). Asylum seekers are not eligible for support for any Higher Education and are classed as overseas students for fee purposes until they have received a positive decision on their asylum application. The net result of these policies is to promote the perception of refugees as a burden on the community, dependent on welfare rather than as an asset to the community. It also, of course, delays the process of rebuilding lives and integrating.

Alongside these measures to control asylum seekers, the Labour government introduced a number of key policy documents setting out the UK integration strategy for refugees. The key policies and proposals are set out in the following documents: *Full and Equal Citizens* (Home Office, 2000), *Integration Matters* (Home Office, 2005), *Working to Rebuild Lives* (DWP, 2005), *The Consultation Paper for A New Model for National Refugee Integration Services in England* (Home Office, 2006b) and *Moving on Together: Government's Recommitment to Supporting Refugees* (Home Office UK Border Agency, 2009a). The concept of integration is contested and there is no generally accepted definition or model of refugee integration. A Home Office review of the literature found over forty definitions of the term (Ager and Strang, 2004). The report proposed a working definition of integration as being when an individual or group:

> ... achieve public outcomes within employment, housing, education, health etc. which are equivalent to those achieved within the wider host communities, and are in active relationship with members of their ethnic or national community, wider host communities and relevant services and functions of the state, in a manner consistent with shared notions of nationhood and citizenship in that society. (Ager and Strang, 2004:9)

It is important to note that asylum seekers have no integration rights or entitlements; the strategy excludes asylum seekers and takes the starting point of the integration process as the time when refugee status is confirmed by the Home Office. This leads to a 'waiting period' for asylum seekers which, despite efforts to speed up the system, can last for many months and in some cases years. The exclusion of asylum seekers from integration strategies has been consistently criticised by organisations working with refugees and asylum seekers. It reinforces the distinction between 'genuine' refugees on the one hand and 'bogus' asylum seekers on the other. It means that for a time asylum seekers are left in limbo, unable to begin the process of resettlement. This delay in accessing training and employment opportunities while their application for asylum is processed can result in loss of skills, confidence and self esteem; the longer the period of inactivity and exclusion from mainstream activities the more difficult the process of integration becomes (Waddington, 2005; Bloch, 2007).

Strategies for integration can be broadly conceptualised as adopting either an assimilationist approach or a multicultural approach, although for many commentators the difference between the two is merely one of degree. The assimilationist approach is based on the assumption that migrants will eventually become fully incorporated into the host society and should not bring about significant social or cultural change to that society. Castles (2003) traces assimilationist views to the Chicago School and the study of inter-group relations in the 1920s. He points to the functionalist assumptions underlying the notion of a society which is not only homogeneous but also harmonious: in order to maintain harmony the migrant must adopt the values, norms and behaviour of the receiving society. The underlying assumption about all migrants is that their pre-migration culture has no value and has to be shed in order to go through a process of 're-socialisation or acculturation' (2003:23). The need for migrants to adopt the dominant culture remains highly influential in policy and political discourses and can be seen, for example, in the more assimilationist policies in France and Germany.

The UK has traditionally been associated with a more liberal or multicultural model of integration characterised by greater tolerance of cultural and ethnic diversity, and by viewing integration as more of a two-way process, with the receiving society having some responsibility to adapt to difference. Where the balance of responsibility between migrant and host is struck, and to what degree commonality and difference are stressed and in what areas of life, have been a source of struggle and contestation. A common criticism of multiculturalism is that it tends to assume that there is a dominant culture which is somehow given, and cultural difference is then defined in terms of 'otherness' or even deviance from this norm.

In response to the social unrest in Bradford, Burnley and Oldham, the Cantle Report (Home Office, 2001) argued that some communities were effectively leading 'parallel lives'. Segregation of communities was damaging and needed to be tackled by a policy framework which encouraged community cohesion. Multiculturalism has come under attack from those who would have been expected to support it. Trevor Phillips, then chair of the British Commission for Racial Equality (renamed the Equality and Human Rights Commission in 2007), highlighted the issue when he controversially claimed that Britain was 'sleepwalking to segregation'. Nick Johnson outlined the Commission's position and argued that there has been too much focus on:

> ... the 'multi' of multiculturalism and not enough on the common culture ... We have emphasised what divides us over what unites us, and tolerance of diversity has led to the effective isolation of communities (Johnson, 2007:25).

Debates around multiculturalism and integration intensified and were steered in a slightly difference direction by the events of September 11, 2001 and the subsequent 'war on terror'. Issues of fear and insecurity began to underpin much of the subsequent debate and response towards minority communities, and in particular Islamic communities (Yuval-Davis *et al*, 2005; Somerville, 2007; Zetter, 2007). These were further inflamed by notions of 'homegrown terrorism' in the wake of the July 2005 bombs in London. These events, coupled with the disturbances in the northern towns in the summer of 2001, challenged the

UK's model of multiculturalism and led to criticisms from both right and left of the political spectrum.

On both the left and the right of politics there has been a growing emphasis on the need to stress shared values and a sense of common culture and identity, rather than difference and diversity. This has been reflected in Government policy which has been adopting an increasingly assimilationist approach to integration. The 2002 White Paper *Secure Borders, Safe Haven* which later emerged as *The Nationality, Immigration and Asylum Act* (2002), was published shortly after the Cantle Report and is underpinned by more general concerns about social cohesion and fragmentation. It sets out the government's concern to develop and strengthen 'a sense of belonging to a wider community', 'common values' and 'shared civic identity to unite around' (Home Office, 2002b:10). In order to achieve this, the White Paper proposed language and 'life in the UK' tests for refugees, along with citizenship ceremonies to mark becoming a British citizen. Since November 2005 all refugees (with a few exceptions such as the very elderly or those with learning difficulties) who wish to apply for British citizenship must pass a citizenship test, swear an oath of allegiance and pass an English language test.

The increasing emphasis on the 'responsibilities' of citizenship, social cohesion and integration has been underlined by subsequent legislation. In 2005 a five year plan was introduced which gives only temporary status for those granted refugee status rather than permanent residency, effectively removing longer term security of refugees. At the end of the five-year period individuals must apply for Settlement Protection (Indefinite Leave to Remain), and a review, to include conditions in the refugee's country of origin, will determine whether or not they can remain in the UK (Home Office, 2005). The 2008 Green Paper: *The Path to Citizenship: next steps in reforming the immigration system* introduced the notion of 'earned citizenship', parts of which later emerged in the 2009 *Borders, Citizenship and Immigration Act.* The paper proposed that refugees (and other migrants) who wished to settle in the UK would need to 'demonstrate a more visible and a more substantial contribution to Britain' (Home Office Border and Immigration Agency, 2008:6). Instead of being able to apply directly for full citizenship after five years refugees would have an additional period of 'probationary citizenship'. This period could be accelerated through volunteering and other demonstrations of 'active citizenship' – or it could be slowed down or halted by 'criminality' (Home Office UK Border Agency, 2009b). The language of 'earning the right to stay' and the extra period of one to three years before refugees receive the security of permanent residency was strongly criticised by the UK Refugee Council. They argue that it runs counter to the spirit of the government's commitment to protect refugees and fulfill its obligations under the Refugee Convention and the European Convention on Human Rights (Refugee Council, 2009). The policy of 'earned citizenship' was due to be implemented in July 2011. However, the new Coalition Government announced at the end of 2010 that it would not go ahead with the proposals as the policy was too complicated and bureaucratic. New proposals are expected to be announced in 2011.

Public discourses and refugees

Particularly since 2001, migrants have come to represent growing concerns about national identity and values; fear of the 'other' and concerns about social relations between newcomers and settled community are often in the media spotlight. Much of the attention has generated negativity and panic towards refugees (Robinson, 2003). Kundnani (2001) argues that negative media coverage has created a climate where racism against refugees can go unrecognised as racism and therefore pass unchallenged. Reporting of asylum issues by UK newspapers is regularly cited by refugee support organisations as one of the biggest problems affecting the quality of life of refugees and asylum seekers in the UK (ICAR, 2004).

Research into public attitudes around asylum conducted by the Independent Asylum Commission (Hobson *et al*, 2008) found that only 18 per cent of people in their survey viewed the term 'asylum' positively. Their research found that the majority of respondents believed that there were:

> ... too many asylum seekers, and too many of them are 'bogus'; asylum seekers tell lies to stay in the country; Britain is a 'soft touch' and takes more than its fair share of asylum seekers; asylum seekers are here to steal jobs and scrounge on welfare; asylum seekers get preferential treatment in the allocation of housing and public services; ... are prioritised over the in-

> digenous population, and are a threat to British culture ... (Hobson *et al*, 2008:14).

It is interesting that very few respondents had had any direct contact with an asylum seeker. Their primary source of information about asylum was the national media followed by local media and 'word of mouth'. The report concluded that overall, the treatment of asylum seekers in the UK fell 'seriously below the standards to be expected of a humane and civilised society'.

Alongside such hostility and marginalisation, refugees have to contend with what Zetter (2007) refers to as bureaucratic labelling processes. He argues that there has been a change in the way in which refugees are labelled. In the past when refugees were largely contained within the 'global South' they were labelled within a humanitarian discourse by Non Governmental Organisations (NGOs) however, as refugees started arriving in large numbers at Europe's borders the labelling role has been assumed by northern governments and used for instrumental purposes. There has been what Zetter calls a fractioning of the refugee label which has transformed 'refugee' from the interpretation of the Geneva Convention and given rise to a proliferation of new and often pejorative labels and sub-labels, including 'genuine refugee', 'asylum seeker', 'bogus asylum seeker' 'dispersed asylum seeker', and a range of labels indicating temporary refugee status (eg. 'Limited Leave to Remain', 'Humanitarian Leave to Remain'). The purpose of the latter categories is to act as 'warehouses' containing entry and restricting access. Zetter argues that there are now a larger number of less privileged labels, some of which, such as those applied to asylum seekers, impose severe restrictions which might force the holder to try and subvert it by, for example, working illegally. It is an example of how state policy effectively criminalises refugees seeking asylum (Zetter, 2007).

Through the bureaucratic labelling process meanings are ascribed and identities are formed and transformed. The asylum seeker label transforms an identity into a politicised image; it is not a neutral way of describing the world, but has the covert intention to

> ... convey an image of marginality, dishonesty, a threat, unwelcomed ... conveying undesirable images of destitution and an unwelcome burden ... (*ibid*: 184 and 185)

The new labels are created in political and policy discourse and represent a 'messy political response' to control the influx of refugees.

> [T]he label 'refugee', and its many subcategories, reflect a political discourse on migration which has deconstructed and reinvented interpretations and meanings in order to legitimise state interests and strategies to regulate migration. Labels reveal the political in the apolitical. (Zetter, 2007:188)

Refugees may move through complex processes of sequential labelling (Zetter, 2007), for example from asylum seeker who may, if their application is unsuccessful be returned to the country they have come from, to refugee with temporary leave to remain, to refugee with indefinite leave to remain. It is only at this final point that refugees can apply for British citizenship, apply for visas for family members to visit or to join them permanently. At each stage refugees have to learn to live with, manage and in some cases subvert the different identities and statuses they are assigned and about which they have no choice.

In later chapters we see how policy and wider social discourses are played out in the lives of refugees, but first I want to explore how we might conceptualise and theorise learning in order to apprehend these experiences from a learning perspective.

3
Perspectives on learning

A great many different approaches and theories attempt to capture the complex set of processes involved in human learning. Each perspective foregrounds different elements of the whole, be it the individual or socio-cultural context, social interaction, formality or informality of context and so on. This chapter examines key ideas and perspectives which provide a backdrop for illuminating the learning and identity processes associated with being a refugee. First though, I consider the rise in interest of the concept of lifelong learning, particularly among policy makers, and how this had led to a shift in focus around adult learning.

Contemporary conditions of globalisation, rapid technological change and information proliferation have, it is suggested, given rise to the focus on lifelong learning (see eg. Field, 2006). The concept implies a view of learning that is no longer solely about an activity which occurs in a classroom or other formal setting, or about the acquisition of a fixed body of knowledge or skills. Rather, learning can be found in many and diverse places, and knowledge and skills will require constant updating.

In its *Memorandum on Lifelong Learning* (2000) the European Commission argued for a 'continuum of learning throughout life', and stated that:

> Lifelong learning is no longer just one aspect of education and training; it must become the guiding principle for provision and participation across the

full continuum of learning contexts. (Commission of the European Communities, 2000:3)

The report gives two reasons why lifelong learning is a priority for the European Union. Firstly, Europe has moved towards a knowledge-based society and economy and its competitiveness depends upon improving the employability and adaptability of its workforce. Secondly, the report recognises the complex social and political world in which we live and the necessity to 'learn to live positively with cultural, ethnic and linguistic diversity' (2000:5). These reasons underpin the joint aims of lifelong learning: promoting employability, and active citizenship. The Memorandum goes on to identify three basic categories of purposeful learning:

- formal learning takes place in education and training institutions, leading to recognised diplomas and qualifications
- non-formal learning takes place alongside the mainstream systems of education and training and does not typically lead to formalised certificates. Non-formal learning may be provided in the workplace and through the activities of civil society organisations and groups ...
- informal learning is a natural accompaniment to everyday life. Unlike formal and non-formal learning, informal learning is not necessarily intentional learning, and so may well not be recognised even by individuals themselves as contributing to their knowledge and skills (2000:8)

The memorandum notes that the concept of lifelong learning draws attention to the temporal nature of learning: learning occurs throughout the life course, continuously or periodically. It draws attention to the spread of learning across various contexts and activities. This 'life-wide' dimension of learning brings the non-formal and informal learning into sharper focus and the distinction between informal and formal learning has become less significant (2000:9). Learning becomes part of our whole life experience and no aspect of life is left untouched by learning.

This shift and the broadening out of the concept of learning in policy reflects growing recognition that formal learning is only a small part of the totality of significant learning and that the informal learning which occurs through transient social interactions may be of much greater significance. Coffield (2000a) used the metaphor of an iceberg to describe informal learning as the 'submerged and neglected world' which is of much greater importance than the smaller visible section representing formal learning (Coffield, 2000a:1). It recognises that for adults their major frame of reference when it comes to learning is from what they have experienced and practised in social groups, from watching others, from TV, from work. It is what Dominice refers to as social learning or adult socialisation (Dominice, 2000).

The moving away from rigid categorisations of informal and formal learning is also welcome. A review of non-formal learning commissioned by the Learning and Skills Research Centre (LSRC) concluded that the terms formal, non-formal and informal were used across the literature in contradictory and contestable ways, and that the terms informal and non-formal learning tended to be used interchangeably. They concluded that it was not possible to conceptualise informal/ non-formal learning as being fundamentally separate from formal learning. Instead it is more sensible to see attributes of informality and formality as being present in all learning situations (Colley *et al*, 2003).

There has been debate as to how 'new' the concept of lifelong learning actually is, or whether it is just a case of re-branding (Boshier, 1998; Borg and Mayo, 2005). Field (2006) argues that although the idea itself can be traced back to the intellectual fervour that followed the end of World War One, it wasn't until the 1990s that lifelong learning emerged onto the policy scene 'with the suddenness of a new fashion' and gained 'global policy consensus' (2006:11-12). He argues that lifelong learning betrays an ambition that he has termed 'the new educational order', in which learning has acquired a new meaning not only for education and training institutions but for individuals and society as a whole. Social scientists Beck and Giddens talk of late- or post-modernity and what they term 'reflexivity', or the need for individuals constantly to reflect on what they know and to make choices about who they are and how they plan and live their lives. Life courses are much less predictable than in the past and a state of permanent learning is an inescapable feature of contemporary modern society which, they argue, is characterised by risk and uncertainty (Giddens, 1991; Beck, 1992).

The contemporary constructions of lifelong learning are not without their critics. It has been argued that lifelong learning represents new forms of domination and governmentality where individuals are expected to be continually renewing their knowledge and skills to meet the rapidly changing needs of the global economy. Field (2006) among others has argued that the habits of self regulation and self-monitoring are shifting inexorably towards the individual. A similar point is made by Griffin (2002), who argues that by focusing on lifelong learning governments are abandoning policies, which focus on the structures of provision, and adopting strategies, which aim to shift to a culture of learning by empowering individuals. The self-motivated, self-regulated and self-policed nature of lifelong learning ensures that it functions as a mechanism of social control and as an alternative to welfare provision. Similar arguments are made by Crowther (2004), and by Martin (2003) who suggests that lifelong learning is being used for the moral regulation of individuals. On a slightly different tack, Coffield (2000b) questions the human capital theory on which lifelong learning policy is built arguing that

> ... for too long lifelong learning has remained an evidence-free zone, under-researched, under-theorised, unencumbered by doubt and unmoved by criticism ... (2000b:4)

What is clear is that, as Edwards and Usher (1998) maintain, the discourse of lifelong learning symbolises a loosening of boundaries around the concept of adult learning and has shifted in focus to the wider processes of learning and to theories of learning which lie beyond those traditionally associated with adult education. Alheit and Dausien (2002 and 2007) refer to the concept of lifelong learning as being double-faced. On the one hand there is the instrumentalising view driven by economic and political imperatives; on the other it 'emancipates' by encouraging the focus on non-formal and informal learning and drawing attention to the learning processes of individual social actors. This has given impetus to a shift in analytical perspective so that boundaries between learning and personal experience become increasingly difficult to draw (eg. Alheit and Dausien, 2002; West, 2001; West *et al*, 2007).

The following sections examine some of the different perspectives on learning, the priorities they address and the assumptions which underpin them.

Learning and experience

Traditionally, much of the theory of adult education drew heavily upon life cycle theory and the concept of andragogy as a way of conceptualising adult education as a distinct field, separate and different from the teaching of children. One of the central assumptions of andragogy, as expressed by Knowles (1970), is that adult hood is a distinct stage of life, characterised by increased self direction and a body of accumulated experience which can be used as a resource for learning. This concept of a stage based model of learning is somewhat undermined if, as has been suggested, life courses in contemporary society are no longer clearly mapped out and predictable. Nonetheless, the idea that the individual's experience is the foundation and most important resource for learning still underlies much of the discourse and assumptions of Western adult education. This emphasis assumes that adults come to learning situations with experience and that this is at the centre of knowledge production and acquisition.

The centrality of the individual's experience is the defining feature of liberal humanist understandings of learning. Its theoretical base is in humanistic psychology and in particular the work of Carl Rogers (1967 and 1980). Coming from a therapeutic background, Rogers made connections between 'client centred' approaches to therapy and 'learner-centred' approaches to learning. He argued that learning is more than a cognitive activity; it has an essential affective and moral dimension and should support the growth of the whole person. It is the whole person who is involved in learning, and learners have to be allowed to be themselves, to be authentic human beings. The liberal humanist perspective expressed in Rogers' ideas on education was particularly popular during the 1960s and 1970s, and the ideas remain influential. In particular the role of the individual's experience in the learning process and the image of the self-directed, autonomous learner still have a powerful presence in both humanist and radical adult education (Usher, Bryant and Johnston, 2002).

The learner in this paradigm has a central role as a meaning maker: interpreting and building frames of reference and constructing knowledge. As Fraser (1995) suggests, the underlying assumption is

> ... of the self as a 'narrator' who can recollect experience and turn it into learning. 'Learning' is understood as a process which operates in any number of formal or informal situations. It is not restricted to scholastic or vocational environments but includes the learning gained from the myriad quotidian experiences we all encounter as we perform the various roles our social obligations demand of us. (1995:x)

Kolb (1984) is probably one of the most well known writers from an experientialist perspective. He defines learning as 'the process whereby knowledge is created through the transformation of experience' (1984: 41). In his famous 'learning cycle', learning occurs through reflection on, and analysis of, concrete experience and abstract knowledge, so that ideas and understanding are constantly being formed and re-formed in a dynamic and fluid process in the light of experience (Kolb, 1984). The notion that learning is the process of transforming experience through reflection is a powerful and influential perspective on learning and has provoked much scholarly exploration. Boud *et al* (1985) for example, have developed an understanding of the reflective process; and in workplace learning the notion of the reflective practitioner has been used to develop a theory of professional action (Schon, 1983 and 1987).

Of particular significance for understanding migration is the work of Jack Mezirow on transformative learning (1990; 2000). Drawing on humanist approaches, his work focuses on situations of disjuncture in individual's lives. He defines transformative learning as:

> ... the process by which we transform our taken-for-granted frames of reference (meaning perspectives, habits of mind, mind-sets) to make them more inclusive, discriminating, open, emotionally capable of change, and reflective so that they may generate beliefs and opinions that will prove more true or justified to guide action ... Transformative Theory's focus is on how we learn to negotiate and act on our own purposes, values, feelings, and meanings rather than those we have uncritically assimilated from others ... (Mezirow, 2000:8)

A central proposition is that when an individual's 'frame of reference' or 'meaning perspective' is discordant with their experience, a 'disorientating dilemma occurs', and individuals begin to critically reflect on and question the validity of their inherited meaning perspective, where upon transformation of perspective can occur. He suggests that learning occurs in one of four ways: by elaborating existing frames of reference; by learning new frames of reference; by transforming points of view; or by transforming habits of mind (2000: 19). The learning processes involve different degrees of comprehension and 'mindfulness'; they may be the result of deliberate enquiry, incidental or 'mindlessly assimilative'. Such transformations can also be sudden or incremental.

Whereas Mezirow's focus is on the individual and personal transformation, Paolo Freire's (1996) work with the poor and socially excluded in Brazil places greater emphasis on the socio-cultural milieu, and is concerned with learning as a means of social transformation. Although Freire similarly placed the experience of the learner at the centre of the learning process, he used it to challenge the privileged position of abstract and theoretical forms of knowing over forms of knowing which are more experiential and personal. His distinction between 'banking' education in which learning is a matter of acquiring the values and culture of the dominant elite, and 'conscientisation' in which the individual constructs their own personal and social meanings from their personal experience, raises important epistemological issues about the nature of knowledge and the social world. The notion of learning as a process of 'banking' knowledge and this conceptualisation of the world relies on an empiricist view of knowledge: that somehow there is a body of objective knowledge 'out there' waiting to be discovered and which can then be broken down and absorbed.

Moreover, Freire reminds us that knowledge is not neutral, impartial or static, but is the product of our socio-historical conditioning and is constructed through the interaction of individuals with each other and with the world (Freire, 1985). The role of the educator is not to by-pass what individuals bring with them in terms of their understanding of the world; rather it is to recognise and respect these knowledges and understandings. This 'local' and 'partial' context is the base from which other knowledge can be built (Freire, 1992). Rejecting the notion that education is about the transference of a neutral body of knowledge, the writings of Freire present education and the production of knowledge as inherently political processes, rooted in relations of power.

Each of the perspectives briefly considered here have, to varying degrees, foregrounded the individual and the role of experience in the learning process. While not ignoring the socio-cultural context as important in the learning process, it has not been their primary focus. The next section looks at theories which instead see learning as a social process, situated in a particular context.

Socio-cultural perspectives on learning

The work of Jean Lave and Etienne Wenger (Lave, 1996 and Lave and Wenger, 1991) has been particularly influential in establishing the essentially social character of learning. Jean Lave, an anthropologist, drew upon her work with apprentice tailors in Liberia, West Africa to develop her ideas of learning (Lave, 1996). Her work challenges the view of informal learning as being narrow and in some way inferior to the learning obtained from formal education.

> I began to enquire into just what was being learned by the apprentices, and found that the apprentices were learning many complex 'lessons' at once. To name a few: they were learning relations among the major social identities and divisions in Liberia and society which they were in the business of dressing. They were learning to make a life, to make a living, to make clothes, to grow old enough and mature enough to become master tailors, and to see the truth of the respect due to a master of their trade. ... This recommended serious scepticism about the assumption that the 'informally' educated should not be able to produce knowledge but only reproduce existing practice. (Lave, 1996: 151-152)

The existence of learning in the absence of teaching not only led Lave to question the assumption that intentional transmission or teaching is necessary for learning to take place, but also to conclude that learning is an integral aspect of social interaction. Their concept of learning as a 'situated activity' rejects conventional theories of learning which see knowledge as acquired and internalised through 'discovery', 'transmission', or 'experienced in interaction'. They argue that this focus on internalisation establishes a marked dichotomy between inside and outside, and ignores important concerns such as the nature of the learner, the world in which they live, and their activity in and with the world. They take a holistic approach to the person as a learner, and focus on the relationship between learning and the social situations in which it occurs. Their concept of learning implies a focus '... on activity in and with the world; and on the view that agent, activity, and the world mutually constitute each other (Lave and Wenger, 1991:33).

This view of learning represents a shift away from cognitive processes and conceptual structures to the kinds of social engagements in which learning takes place. The central defining characteristic of their theory of learning as a situated activity is a process of 'legitimate peripheral participation' whereby learning occurs through centripetal participation in communities of knowledge and practice. Newcomers initially participate by both absorbing and being absorbed in the culture of practice. Over a period of legitimate peripherality they gradually assemble an understanding of what constitutes the practice of the community. This might include, for example, the various different roles of those involved, how people conduct their lives and interact, how 'masters' talk, walk and work. As the learner moves centripetally towards full participation in the community of practice and becomes an old timer, the community of practice is reproduced over time.

Their concept of legitimate peripheral participation 'decentres' the view of a teacher or master as pedagogue and instead emphasises the importance of belonging and practice to learning. The analysis of learning centres on how the community's learning resources are structured and accessed: learning cannot be analysed apart from the social relations that shape legitimate peripheral participation. Key to legitimate peripheral participation is access to the community of practice and all that membership entails; to become a full member requires access to opportunities for participating in the social relations and production process, engaging with the artefacts and technologies of everyday practice and understanding their significance.

The contributions of Lave and Wenger provide the basis for a comprehensive social theory of learning which offers the potential to understand and analyse the social positions and roles which individuals occupy as they move through their lives. The emphasis is not so much on the context or learning environment but on the social practices through which individuals learn, and in particular the social relations. How do social relations (not only teachers, friends and family) impact on individuals' ability to participate and move centripetally towards full participation? And what are the barriers? This reconceptualisation of learning with a temporal aspect is particularly important in times of continued social and personal change and development; it is perhaps particularly significant for refugees who are confronted with new and unfamiliar social environments in which they have to participate, and learn rapidly to adapt to.

Some aspects of the learning process are left in the background and not explicitly addressed in Lave and Wenger's work. For example, it does not provide an explicit view of power and how this might manifest itself in social practices and access to the resources of a community of practice. Also, while their concept of learning involves an explicit focus on the person and on the construction of identities (1991:52-53), there is little exploration or theorisation of the concept of the individual or of identity: rather it is taken as self evident (Sfard and Prusack, 2005). Like other social theories of learning it also raises the question of how we integrate and theorise issues of the individual learner; that is, how individual dispositions, values and sense of identity are brought to and impact upon the learning environment, and in turn how learning impacts on the individual's identity and life. Biographical or life course approaches to learning can be seen as just such an attempt to transcend the dichotomy between wider social forces and the individual.

The Biographical turn

Chamberlayne *et al* (2000) describe the turn to biographical methods in social science as partly a response to the dominance of determinism and social constructionism in social science which had led to it becoming detached from lived realities. In contrast, the biographical turn gives greater prominence to personal and social meanings. It recognises that personal accounts of experience can reveal new insight and understanding which had hitherto been ignored or dismissed as inconsequential.

The growth of biographical and life history approaches to the processes of adult learning are part of this broader trend but, as Armstrong (1987) and others have pointed out, the roots of life history work can be traced back further to Thomas and Znaniecki's 1918 pioneering work on immigration and cultural identity, *The Polish Peasant in Europe and America.* Generally recognised as foundational in life history methods and approaches, it was the first work to advocate a position in which both individual and social factors must always be taken into account in any social study: 'the cause of a social or individual phenomenon is never another social or individual phenomenon alone, but always a combination of a social and an individual phenomenon' (Thomas and Znaniecki, quoted in Plummer, 2001:105).

Life history methodology developed within the theoretical orientation of symbolic interactionism in the 1920s and 1930s in the Chicago School of Sociology (Armstrong, 1987). Symbolic interactionists highlight the symbolic and interactive nature of reality and its social construction; their concern is with how individuals make sense of their worlds and act accordingly through social interaction with others. The affinity with life history is exemplified in the work of Faraday and Plummer (1979):

> The life history technique is grounded in a pragmatist approach to knowledge in which the ultimate test of truth is experience. The life history technique and its ally, symbolic interactionism, are not so much concerned with grasping the totality either of structures or personality as they are concerned with depicting the immediate lived experience as actual members in every day society grasp them. These experiences shift and change from context to context, and the criterion of truth here is the grasping objectively of these lived experiences. Hence one may be objective in one's portrait of any world view, but this is not to say that this worldview makes any claim to being any kind of universal truth. (Quoted in Armstrong, 1987:5)

In later work Plummer (2001) has pointed to the broad affinity between some of the themes of post-modern thought and symbolic interactionism. These include respect for multiple perspectives rather than one single privileged 'truth', local and contextual studies rather than grand narratives, emphasis on disorder and flux as opposed to order and continuity (Plummer, 2001:12-13).

In educational research the term 'learning career' was first utilised by Bloomer (1997) and Bloomer and Hodkinson (2000 and 2002). It is based on the idea that individual students agentically construct their own learning through interactions with college-based experiences and interactions with teaching. This experience of being a learner has a longitudinal dimension in that approaches to learning and learner identity develop and change over time. In later work (Hodkinson *et al*, 2007), the term 'learning careers' is replaced with 'learning lives', as this, they argue, more accurately reflects the importance of informal learning and learning as part of everyday practices rather than a separate process. The term 'learning careers' also has connotations that learning is a unilinear process with a clear trajectory, and that changes in identity are permanent rather than contingent and fragile (Crossan *et al,* 2003).

Although these biographical approaches foreground educational and learning processes at the individual level, they emphasise the importance of the external structures that frame the life course. Social, cultural and economic structures, our inheritance from the past all impact on our personal experience, how we interpret, understand and define our social world. The learning processes of an individual cannot therefore be fully understood without reference to their past, or to the social axes of class, gender, age and ethnicity which shape the life course, life plans and aspirations.

Alheit and Dausien (2007) put forward the concept of the 'biographicity of social experience' as a tool for understanding learning at the level both of the individual and the social. This suggests that how learners construct their lives contains hidden references to the structural limitations imposed by social class, ethnicity, gender and so on, so that lives are constructed between the twin poles of structure and subjectivity (Alheit and Dausien, 2007). Learning is always tied to a specific biography and at the same time learning is the precondition for the construction and modification of biography: 'Without biography there can be no learning, without learning, no biography' (Alheit and Dausien, 2002:15).

Learning and identity

Assumed in all of these approaches to learning is an understanding of the learner as a whole person. Body, mind and emotions are intrinsic to the construction and transformation of life experiences which then become integrated into the individual's biography. It is through the integration of learning that the self is constructed and identity is transformed. Lave and Wenger encapsulate this in the idea of centripetal movement in a community of practice from newcomer or novice to full membership and competence. Learning is a lifelong, life wide process; it is an essential part of being human and an essential way in which identity is constructed and changed. Implicit is the sense that learning is about change for the better, and that somehow it is always a good thing. Jarvis for example suggests that learning '... plumbs the depth of human existence-in-the-world. We are always both being-in-the-world and becoming, developing, growing, maturing' (2007:14). Hodkinson *et al* (2007) similarly propose a view of learning as being about the construction of the self '... people become through learning, and learn through becoming' (Hodkinson *et al*, 2007:33). They argue that by conceptualising learning as part of being, and also part of the ongoing construction of the person, learning, identity and agency are interwoven in people's lives such that there is no clear separation between them.

This chapter has noted the shift in both policy and research towards learning as being a lifelong and life wide process. Insights offered by the different perspectives outlined here suggest a lens through which to explore the experience of transition from one social and learning milieu to another. Drawing on a biographical approach enables the situating of migration within the broader framework of individuals' life histories: the social and cultural experiences which shaped their lives before they came to the UK, and how these now impinge on and influence their experience of life in the UK. In turn the different social world offered in the UK becomes integrated into individual biography, involving the (re)construction of identity and sense of self. The emphasis on social interaction, participation and transformation usefully highlight the informal learning and meaning making which occurs in social encounters and as part of everyday practices in any location, including formal learning contexts. It is an approach which recognises learning as an inevitable part of life. It has not only a temporal aspect to learning but also a focus on social positions, agency and the construction of identities.

4

Maryam: the Iraqi teacher's story

When we met, Maryam had been in the UK for four years. Her narrative emphasises the enormous amount of identity work that can occur prior to migration and the length of time it can take to start to re-establish a professional identity. The struggle to be reunited with her children and her husband had dominated her first years here, and it was only when the family was finally reunited that she turned her thoughts to the possibility of re-training in the UK and doing anything other than unskilled work. During her time in the UK she has taken a number of courses to prepare herself for entry into higher education and teacher training. She has also had to renegotiate her role and identity as a mother.

One of the things that had always struck me about Maryam was her positive approach to life in the UK. She was unstintingly cheerful and happy with her life, no matter what difficulties and problems she and her family faced. Her narrative illustrates her determination to fit in and become a part of UK society and culture. It is only when we learn of her life in Iraq and the struggles that she and her family have endured that we can make sense of her approach and disposition. Her life story before she came to the UK is explored in some detail as it is pertinent to her narrative in the UK. Perhaps more than any of the other stories, Maryam's underlines the importance and value of a life history approach because it illustrates how, if we don't have the biographical and cultural understanding of her life in Iraq, we cannot understand her present.

Life in Iraq

Maryam was born in Iraq in 1960, the youngest of seven children. She describes education as being very important in her family; her father and five of her siblings were teachers. Her father ensured that she attended the best primary and secondary schools and she received extra tuition and support at home, so that when she was at school she felt 'better than the others'. She easily completed primary and secondary school, and moved to university where she studied mechanical engineering and education.

The Ba'thist coup in 1968 initially caused little change to the lives of Maryam and her family; indeed Maryam probably benefited from the Ba'ath Party's gender ideology and policies at first. In the early days of the party's rule, the emancipation of women was key to their plans to transform Iraq into a modern and productive state (Al-Ali, 2007:131). Women were encouraged to enrol in universities and professional schools, and to enter the labour market alongside men (Rassam, 1992). The result was that Iraqi women became among the most educated and professional in the region (Al-Ali, 2007:138). By 1980, women accounted for 46 per cent of all teachers, 29 per cent of physicians, 46 per cent of dentists, and 70 per cent of pharmacists (Al-Khalil, 1989:88).

During her four year degree course Maryam was approached by the Ministry of Education, who offered her financial support during her degree if she worked for them on graduation. She took up their offer and worked for fifteen years as a teacher of mechanical engineering. She married and had three children. She describes how it was easy to combine parenting with working, as the teaching day was short (8am to 12 noon), and they had long holidays.

It was a time when the Iraqi Government was actively encouraging and supporting women in the labour market. The oil boom in 1973 had led to great economic expansion during the 1970s; faced with labour shortages, the Iraqi Government needed educated women to fill the gaps. This was the 'golden age' of a flourishing economy, expanding middle class and state-led development (Al Ali, 2007). For women like Maryam, it translated into generous state provision and support which included free nursery provision and transportation to and from schools and workplaces. Alongside this, Maryam lived with her mother-in law, who helped with childcare. She returned to work just forty days after the birth of her sons and six months after the birth of her daughter.

Maryam describes the teaching profession then as one of the best jobs in Iraq. As a teacher she and her family were well respected and well paid. She felt passionate about education and derived great satisfaction from her work. However, alongside the prospering socio-economic conditions in Iraq, the Ba'ath Party promoted feelings of paranoia, xenophobia and distrust, not only towards external enemies, but also towards internal ethnic and religious minority groups (Davis, 2005). The process of marginalisation of social groups and sectarianism deepened and accelerated during the 1970s. In order to create and maintain cultural and political boundaries, the regime gave increasing attention to 'cultural authenticity' (*asil*), and determining who could be part of the Iraqi political community. Those who were deemed to reside outside of it included Shi'i Arabs, Kurds, Jews and those with real, or alleged, Iranian nationality. They faced brutal repression, deportation, and exclusion from national political and cultural discourse (2005). Al Ali (2007) suggests that during the 'time of deportation' (*zamn-al tas-firat*) hundreds of thousands of Shi'i were forced to leave Iraq because of their alleged Iranian nationality (*tabaiya iraniya*) (Al Ali, 2007; Al Khalil, 1989).

The cause of Maryam's family's difficulties stemmed from her father's Iranian heritage. He had been born in Iran and moved to Iraq when he was three years old. She describes the process of persecution:

> They started with the common people, I mean with the merchants and they deported them from Iraq. But with the teachers, with the others, they didn't start until, my brother he was a teacher at medical school, they told him to move from teaching. I don't remember which year ... 1980. And then little by little my other brother, he was a maths teacher they told him he had to leave and my sister, she was a teacher of English. She said I am not going to stay as a teacher, I don't want to work with them, so she already had 25 years so she took retire[ment]. It affected us all, but my father he was already retired, it doesn't affect him. In 1982 they said it is not allowed for you to stay in Iraq, they tried to deport him but I don't know, they took him for one month with my mother and my brother ...

Maryam's elderly father was eventually left alone, but for the rest of the family things got progressively more difficult, particularly after 1979 when Saddam Hussein became president. Within a year Iraq was at war with its neighbour Iran (1980-1988). In 1982, the Ba'ath Party passed a law offering financial reward to Iraqi men who divorced their Iranian wives (Abdullah, 2003, cited in Ali Ali, 2007:157). Maryam's husband, who was an engineer in the Iraqi air force, refused to divorce her and was dismissed from the air force and lost all the privileges it had afforded him and his family.

Control of the education system was a specific focus of the regime, as schools and colleges were seen as key sites for the indoctrination of the young. Teachers were under particular pressure (Al-Ali, 2007; Al-Khalil, 1989). The content of education and who could teach became the subject of scrutiny and rapid change, and so did the question of who could be admitted to educational institutions. In 1978 it was decreed that all personnel of the armed forces, internal security and public intelligence forces should be admitted to universities, colleges and schools regardless of 'academic achievement, period of enrolment, and attendance' (Al-Khalil, 1989:103). Pressure was placed on teachers to allow students to cheat in exams, to accept bribes and to give high marks to certain students. Maryam describes the degradation of the education system and, with it, the teaching profession:

> Till 1980 it was very perfect, but when the war started and the people they didn't care about the education because of the war. Their children they were going to go to war and you hear everyone everyday: someone died, he studied, he worked very hard in studying and then the Government send him to the war and he didn't come back. So the people gradually they didn't care about education and especially Saddam, he didn't like educated people so he didn't care. ... He said the mother who gives birth [to] more [than] four children she will get more support [than] the mother if she had two or three children. They respect the family that have four children and above, four, five, six than the family who have one, two or three they are not respectable, so they didn't get support because they want the woman to give birth, they want people for war. So he didn't care about education and he started to make the salary less ... Even at University if you work with Ba'ath Party you will get a lot of support from the Government with your degree, with your mark, you will get a high mark. If you want to go to better University you will get higher mark if your father or your family from Ba'ath Party. Everything he does made education lower and lower and lower ...The student gets more money that the teacher, so the teacher had to respect the student, the students don't respect the teacher, no.

For Maryam, fairness and integrity were at the heart of teaching and her self-respect as a teacher. She was in an intolerable position when she knew that colleagues were allowing students to cheat, or when the head teacher ordered her to falsify class registers to ensure that certain students were always marked as present. The gradual erosion of her professional status and identity as a teacher was accompanied, as she suggests, by a shift in gender ideology.

During the 1980s the ideology and rhetoric around women began to change as more young men were needed to fight the numerically superior Iranian army. Al-Ali (2007) describes how women's roles became redefined from 'producers to reproducers' and gender ideology shifted to the 'glorification of the Iraqi mother'. Towards the mid to late 1980s the regime launched a fertility campaign, encouraging women to have five or more children. For Maryam this meant that the school caretaker who had ten children, and could neither read nor write, had a higher salary and commanded more respect than the teachers at the school.

After fifteen years of teaching, Maryam, like her older brothers and sisters, was finally forced to leave her job in 1993. She describes teaching as the only job she ever wanted to do and, rather than take an alternative more menial job, she chose to stay at home with her children and do private or 'contract' teaching work. So many teachers had been 'retired' from teaching that there was a shortage and she was allowed back on short term contracts to cover the shortages.

The Ba'ath Party regime reconfigured the policy, discursive and ideological framework in Iraq such that mechanisms of valuation and objective conditions were dramatically changed over a very short time. Looked at in Bourdieu's framework, changes in the field meant that social positions such as teacher, which had appeared secure and valued, were downgraded and disparaged. New classifying practices such as 'pure' and 'impure' were used to mark habitus and subsequently functioned as markers of exclusion and inclusion. Maryam's capital and habitus now held different meaning across different fields of interaction: they were ill adapted and had little purchase in the new conditions and demands of the social field.

Maryam describes how they waited, hoping that their situation in Iraq would improve, but why they eventually took the decision that they had to leave:

> [It was] becoming worse and worse. ... Even in 1991 we were very happy, I mean we thought Saddam will be ruined and be finished and he came back again. So gradually it start[ed] to affect our children ... if you want to go education it is not allowed, College of Education, College of Sport not allowed, and if you want to be as their father in the army it is not allowed. I thought, oh it means they will get in the same situation as me ... I don't want one day [that] they will take them and we will never see them. Because it is very easy; they know we hate Saddam in [our] house and if they by mistake say it, we will never see them [again]. And we put them in very good schools which they have most of the Government sons with them and I was very frightened every day. I think if they make ... in front of them we try our best not to show anything that we hate them but they know the situation: I've been retired, their father retired because of the Government and we were very frightened. In 1999 my son he got to A-Level and after that he had to go to University and I told them nothing at all [will] change – they will be in the same situation getting worse and worse, I don't want to lose them and we decided to go, 1999.

By the time Maryam finally left Iraq she had lived through years of insidious persecution, she and her family had been gradually excluded from social, political and economic life. Only her three older siblings who were by then in their sixties and seventies remained in Iraq; the three younger ones, like her, sought refuge in other countries. Her identity and that of her family had been gradually eroded and transformed from respectable middle class teachers to a 'culturally impure' family because of their Iranian heritage. Unlike mass migration caused by a specific humanitarian emergency, the onset of migration was for her a gradual process, eventually triggered by fear for the safety and future of her children. It illustrates the complexity of present day migration and how minority groups can suffer human rights abuses and persecution over a protracted period of time before finally leaving (Zetter, 2007).

Maryam's journey out of Iraq was traumatic and deeply stressful. She first went to Jordan with her sons, aged seventeen and fifteen, and her daughter aged seven. Her husband's military background made it more difficult and dangerous for him to leave, so he stayed behind, planning to try and join them once they were safe. Originally she had intended to try and find work as a teacher in a neighbouring Arab country, but she was told that it would be too hard for a woman without a husband to settle and find work. In the end she decided to try and join her brother in the UK. However, the British Embassy in Jordan would only grant a visa for her and not her children. At that time she had no idea of how the immigration system worked, or that she could apply for asylum in the UK, and then apply for her children to join her.

> I didn't know anything about that, because when you are in Iraq everything is a block, you don't know anything about the other world.

Even her brother, who had been granted refugee status in the UK six years earlier, did not dare to tell his family back in Iraq how the asylum system worked, for fear that it would further endanger their lives. In the end her husband sold the family house to raise enough money to pay for the illegal documents for Maryam and their daughter to get to the UK.

> You have to wait, you give the money, this is the first thing. They took the money, and you have to wait until they told you, 'Prepare yourself tomorrow' ... I was waiting for eight months in Jordan, another country, not in my country. And you don't know until they tell you this is your passport ... and I recognise and think it is not a real passport. I thought he will give me a real passport, but he gave me a false one, I didn't know.

The false travel documents were discovered in Qatar, where Maryam and her daughter were held in custody for three days before the Qatari security forces eventually decided to let them continue to the UK. Once in the UK, Maryam received her refugee status quickly and immediately applied for her sons, who were now back to Iraq, to join her. It took six months before the younger son travelled to Jordan and from there could join his mother in the UK. But the older son was eighteen by then and his movements from Iraq were more restricted. It took a year, which entailed stays in Dubai and Yemen, and a legal battle with the Home Office to prove that he had been seventeen when his mother was granted refugee status, before he was finally able to come to the UK. Once her children were all safely in the UK, her husband left Iraq to join them. Although Maryam had obtained all the necessary paperwork for him to join her in the UK as a refugee, it took three years of battling with the bureaucracy of the British Embassies in the region to find an embassy that would provide him with a visa. For Maryam, this was a further trial of her strength and energy, as she emailed and petitioned the embassies, and even made a trip to Syria in the hope of persuading the embassy there to accept his case.

Learning and living in the UK

Maryam had already experienced profound changes in her identity and working life while she was still in Iraq. Her experience of having to travel illegally with false documents, and the long struggle to be reunited with her sons and husband, were deeply stressful experiences. These life events have framed her attitude and approach to settling in the UK. When I asked Maryam about her life in the UK in our earlier interviews, she always emphasised the positive aspects of her experience, the safety, the human rights and the respect that the UK offered. Asked what her expectations had been when she arrived, she replied:

> The first thing it was just peace and all the family together. Just peace and all the family together, to enjoy. This was the main thing, then I started thinking about myself.

She knew when she left Iraq that she would never go back, and that whichever country she ended up in, she would adapt to that culture and make it her home.

> So when I arrived here I didn't think about UK, any European country I will reach I will be melted with them, I will grow, I will try my best to grow my children and to live like them in peace, this is what I think. So when I reached England I think I need to know everything about this culture, I need to be a good person as I was, and continue to work hard in the other country. This is I feel, this is my home, this is. I never thought that I am going to go back.

On some level she knew what to expect because she had been to Europe and the USA as a tourist in the 1970s, but it was different on a practical level when you have to engage with and find your way around the system.

> It is different when you live in a country and you go as a tourist. As a tourist you see all the nice things, you go to watch, to see different life but you

> don't need to be melted with their culture ... but when you want to live you have to know everything about their culture, about their system, about everything in the life. So it was everything new. Although my brother had been here ... it is still much different than when you hear something and when you do it practically.

Everything was so new and different that Maryam felt it was impossible to compare with Iraq. She describes Iraq as being 'very, very strict, we didn't know anything about outside. Politics, culture are forbidden'. Despite the emphasis on the education and employment of women, conservative and patriarchal values prevailed, particularly in relation to traditional gender ideology and relations within the family (Al Ali, 2007). However, movement to a new social space opened up possibilities for her to reflect on the social practices and discourses through which the self had been constituted. For Maryam, migration led to the exposing to critical scrutiny and examination established gendered ways of thinking and being, She found it strange that in the UK women could express opinions and make choices about how you wished to live without fear.

> You cannot say anything in Iraq – it is all for the man, everything ... Here you feel you are free, you can say if you don't like this one or you like that, but in Iraq it is not allowed, especially for the woman ... There you have especially the woman to sacrifice herself for the family. ... But here it is much easier, you can say: 'This is my life'. Nobody blames her, even if she has kids they say this is her life ...

In Maryam's narrative, a recurrent theme was having the right sort of social and cultural capital to navigate around a very different and unfamiliar system of education. In our earlier interviews she talked of the difficulties and frustrations of trying to engage with the school system, firstly with her son and later with her daughter. She found it a particularly difficult system to understand after the rigid and compulsory school curriculum and system of Iraq. The idea that from the age of fourteen, children choose which subjects they wish to study struck her as particularly strange and confusing.

Having recently arrived, Maryam had no social networks and contacts with either the education system or other parents to help her. The idea that social capital and links with wider society are a resource which can bring advantage to those that possess them, as discussed in chapter one, did not apply. While refugee communities may be rich in 'bonding' social capital, they are often excluded from the 'bridging' social capital and the learning within them which is vital for accessing wider social resources. By virtue of having recently arrived in a new culture, refugees, like other marginalised groups, do not tend to have access to the social and cultural capital which can help ensure educational success, either for themselves or for their children.

Because Maryam did not know the system, her son took options at sixteen which were inappropriate to his needs and her aspirations for him. She explained how on arrival her son went straight into year eleven of school and six months later took his GCSE exams. He got E and F grades, but because he had received a letter informing him that he had passed all his GCSEs, Maryam assumed that he would automatically pass on to the next stage of the academic elevator and eventually to university. She didn't know that four passes at A-C grade were required to pass to 'A' levels. When the school suggested a GNVQ in leisure and tourism, she assumed it was the next step towards university and agreed. Maryam describes this as a wasted year for her son; he had no interest in or aptitude for the subject and subsequently left school to find employment.

In the field of the UK education system, Maryam's social and cultural capital had no purchase and could not be employed. The habitus which had been advantageous to her in Iraq, by for example enabling her to ensure that her children went to the best schools, did not equip her for the system here. The disjuncture as she realised that the forms of social and cultural capital she possessed did not enable her to '... wield the power, and influence, and thus to exist, in the field under consideration' (Bourdieu, 1992:98) forced her to renegotiate her identity in relation to her children's education. From being teacher and 'expert' with a clear parental role, she became 'novice', dependent upon them to interpret the system and make decisions for themselves. It meant rethinking family roles and had been hard, but it was a shift which she felt was part of the process of adapting to her new role and their new life in the UK.

> I mean the family it is their responsibility to make the child, to support them to graduate from University and to work or to study hard. But here he

> had to depend on himself. So the first six [months] or one year I thought: 'Oh I have to support him, I have to push him to study', and I tried my best. It didn't work, he said: 'I don't like it', and when you melt in the culture you feel that it is his life, he has to live the life as he wants it, not as I want. And he said: 'I want to leave [school]', I said: 'I don't like it but it is up to you'. But before if I was in Iraq I would never have allowed him. And he said: 'I want to work', and he started work.

Her daughter's experience was different because she arrived in the UK young enough to complete several years of primary school before moving to secondary school. Maryam felt that she was constantly learning from her daughter, who knew more than she did about the school system and which subjects she should study. Candappa and Egharevba (2002) talk of the shifts in the 'inter-generational contract' which can occur in refugee families. In the case of Maryam's family the children did not appear to take on caring and domestic responsibilities within the family, which is not unusual when parents are working long hours and have no support from extended family. They did, however, assume the role of cultural and linguistic translators and brokers. For Maryam, it was a disruption in traditional family roles and drove her to new learning processes. Most of her daughter's homework was done on computers and involved skills and knowledge which Maryam did not possess. It was a far cry from Iraq, where she would spend several hours a night helping and supporting her children with their school work. The habitus which in Iraq equipped her for decoding the social world and managing the fields she encountered did not have value in the UK. This disjuncture engendered an underlying sense of powerlessness, heard in her story.

Once her children were all safely in the UK, Maryam started to look for employment. She had assumed that she would work in a similar profession to that in Iraq. But her Iraqi qualifications in teaching and engineering were not recognised in the UK and she was advised that she would have to start from scratch – as if she had no previous qualifications or experience.

> I didn't know the system, what to do, where to go. I wanted to teach. I asked many people. One person told me to start again; that would take four years: three years undergraduate degree and one year teaching qualification. My degree from Iraq is equivalent to HND here, because it is engineering I

would need to start at year one of an undergraduate course. That's not very good for me to start over again at university, particularly with the family and at my age. It's humiliating for me, what would my family say? They wouldn't understand why I had to start over again.

Maryam's words highlight her bitter disappointment when she realised that the habitus and cultural capital that had enabled her to achieve professional, economic and social success in Iraq was not valued in the UK. It also points to the links with social capital and the difficulties refugees face in navigating around unfamiliar and very different systems of education.

For six months Maryam went to the Job Centre every two weeks, hoping to find a job as either an engineer or a teacher. In the end the advisor suggested that she look at other jobs.

There were other jobs there. She said many people like me work in homes looking after people or there are many jobs cleaning. I didn't want to work looking after people. I got a job in a dry cleaners. ... It's a family run business; they've been very good to me ... they're very nice people.

Although Maryam regarded the job as rather menial because it didn't require any education or qualifications, she enjoyed it. Unlike her experience of teaching in Iraq, she felt she was treated with respect.

Here [the UK] you are in a place where everybody respects you. I was a mechanical engineer, I was a teacher in a secondary school, but I never felt as much respect as I get here. Even my work now, my job, which is without education, anyone can do it. But still, the respect, I get it from my boss and the others, more than I got it from where I was a teacher. Because here human rights are important, and they're respected. There, they don't have any respect. Here you can feel human, you have rights, and everybody respects the rights.

Maryam continued to work at the dry cleaners although she never gave up the dream of returning to teaching. When we discussed teaching during our interviews she joked at times that she would eventually do it 'when I am seventy maybe!'

Through the WILAW programme, Maryam did eventually locate a route into teaching which did not entail starting at year one of an undergraduate degree. She applied for and was offered a place on mathematics education with qualified teaching status undergraduate degree course, as long as she passed English GCSE. After a delay of a year while Maryam put her own study plans on hold to support her daughter who was experiencing difficulties at secondary school, she successfully completed her English GCSE and took her International English Language Test System exam (IELTS), which is a requirement to enter HE in the UK. In 2007, seven years after arriving in the UK she started the two year undergraduate degree.

The first year of the degree in mathematics education focused on developing the fundamental principles and structures of mathematics, an area which she was relatively comfortable with and which enabled her to draw upon her previous experience. The second year was much harder as it involved placements at secondary schools and focused more on educational practices in the UK. Despite the different educational systems and professional practices, Maryam seemed undaunted by the challenges of teaching in the UK. Issues of discipline or difficulties engaging students in the subject were brushed aside; her main concern, she said, was to make her lessons enjoyable.

Maryam has successfully completed her degree and is now teaching in a secondary school. Her journey into higher education was long, because she had to improve her English language and meet the course requirement of GCSE English. Like many other adult and non-traditional learners, her journey was also interrupted by external factors, in her case the needs of her family. Her story draws attention to the importance of specialist advice and information for refugees on how to requalify and top-up qualifications, rather than starting at the beginning. It also highlighted the importance and availability of higher level English language courses, such as IELTS.

Maryam's biography enables us to better understand the identity strategies she has adopted in the UK. Persecution in Iraq, a traumatic flight to the UK and a three year struggle to be reunited with her husband interlace and help to explain her apparent contentment at working for many years at a fairly menial occupation, and her positive disposition and attitude to life in the UK. Having lived with fear for so long and having experienced the degrading of the teaching profession, and ultimately her exclusion from it, her narrative emphasises the freedom from persecution, and her experience of equality and respect in the UK. Battling to find a way for her husband to leave the Middle East and join her, living in safety with her family and supporting her children as best she could, took precedence and priority over re-establishing her career and identity as teacher.

Interestingly, the label and identity of refugee did not feature strongly in Maryam's narrative. Instead the emphasis was on the UK having offered her and her family safety and sanctuary. Maryam had no intention of ever returning to Iraq and it was something she could never imagine changing her mind about. Her life and the lives of her family (both her sons had married and settled in the UK) were firmly established here. Her narrative illustrates how individuals may feel displaced before their eventual flight and challenges the binary of 'home' and 'exile' (Castles, 2003).

5

Patricia: the Zimbabwean teacher's story

Like Maryam, Patricia was a teacher before she came to the UK. This chapter explores narratives around working and learning in the UK. It also charts Patricia's struggle with motherhood: first, as separated from her children and feeling the identity of mother slipping away, and then being reunited and negotiating the differences between what it means to be a middle class mother in Zimbabwe, and what it means to be a mother in the UK.

Some aspects of Patricia's 'biographically acquired landscape of knowledge' (Alheit and Dausien, 2002:15) have transferred and are relevant to the UK context, for example her educational capital and consequent confidence around formal learning, which has been an important source of self. In other ways the process of migration marks a rupture in biographicity, precipitating profound new learning and identity changes, for example around motherhood and paid employment. Her story illuminates how gender, race, class, educational background and other concerns such as worker and economic provider intersect and collaborate to provide the sources for identity construction and self-narration.

Life in Zimbabwe

Patricia was brought up in Zimbabwe, the eldest of eight children. Her mother was a primary school teacher and her father was a head teacher. She describes the value attached to education and the high standards of discipline expected in school.

> Education was very, very important. You had to be educated to be somebody. So they [parents] obviously didn't want you to obtain education which is equal to them, they want you to do much better. So expectation was always high.

After primary school she attended a 'Group A' boarding school which before independence had been a 'Whites only' school. She was one of the first Black children to attend the school and was very much in the minority. Patricia loved boarding school and being away from home. She also enjoyed the sense of being better than the children who attended the former 'Group B' schools and who spoke Shona rather than English at school.

> Yeah, so I also had that experience of speaking English all the time, all the time. So it was nice, it was a good experience ... It kind of made a difference between us and the former Group B schools who didn't speak as much English as we did. Of course they understood it, they read it, everything, but they just weren't as good as we were so we wanted that, we liked that.

At eighteen Patricia started a three year teacher training course. She compared the material and non-material benefits and advantages of the teaching profession:

> It is very respected as a job because everybody knows you have to go through training ... We had two homes, one provided by school where we would be most of the term, then we had our own house where we would go to in the holiday. So it was almost a luxury which some professions didn't have. We didn't need transport because we lived at school. Break time, teatime, lunchtime we would go home and have tea. ... I could always go home and feed the baby and come back, so the convenience was there for teachers, and we had these five-week holidays.

Patricia worked as a primary school teacher in Zimbabwe for eleven years. She married and had three children. As was usual among professional classes in Zimbabwe, Patricia returned to work after the birth of her babies, employing one and at times two maids to care for the children and the home. She describes her life style as being 'luxurious'; she could dedicate herself to her teaching work while leaving all the domestic work to the maids.

> Of course the maids would have two or three weeks off during the holidays to go away. So that was the two or three weeks that I was alone with my chil-

> dren. But otherwise I never had the chance to actually run the home myself or run the house myself and make sure the children had eaten. And sometimes I would do the washing maybe three days before the maid came back because I didn't want her to find loads and loads of washing [laughing]. What impression do you give if you are always saying 'Oh do this, do that' and then you don't do it yourself!

Her life history in Zimbabwe, with its emphasis on education achievement and her positive disposition to learning were an important source of self which she draws upon when confronted with racial prejudice in the UK.

Learning and living in the UK

Patricia came to the UK in August 2002, part of the latest of three waves of migration from Zimbabwe since independence in 1980 (Bloch, 2008). The latest migrants have come to the UK in the context of the ever deepening political and economic crisis and are part of the exodus of professional and middle classes from the country (McGregor, 2007). Patricia arrived on her own, leaving her husband and three children who were then aged twelve, seven and five in Zimbabwe.

When she first arrived in the UK she had assumed that she would continue her profession as a teacher. She compared its teaching salaries with what she was earning in Zimbabwe and thought that she'd 'be very rich in a very short time!' But her Zimbabwean teaching qualifications were not recognised in the UK. One of the routes to gaining Qualified Teaching Status (QTS) involved finding employment in a school and then apply for the Overseas Trained Teacher Programme (OTTP). As we see in chapter eleven, this is a difficult route into teaching for refugees. Having tried to get a placement in one school and observing some lessons, she decided against re-training.

> ... initially when I came I was actually excited about doing the teaching because, because I didn't have any other skills. So I thought well teaching is going to be it. So, and then I realised that although I had a diploma I couldn't really use it here, I had to do two years I think or a year in a school and it wasn't easy to get in a school. I did try, I did try, somebody was helping me and I just went to observe one school but they didn't really need anybody to come in and do any kind of placement there, or they didn't want anybody really. ... And, and then I, well maybe I didn't try hard enough

> really, and after my observation, unfortunately I went to a school that was not very, the discipline wasn't so good, so it wasn't really motivating, it didn't really, say, make me want to do it. So I thought well, I did a bit of catering through an agency, weddings and all that. I did a bit of care, it was just both really, catering and care, catering and care.

It took two years for her children and husband to get permission to join her in the UK. Her strategy during these first years on her own was to work extraordinarily hard. She not only wanted to earn as much money as she could, but found that working long hours helped her to deal with the pain of separation from her family. She describes how she could have three, sometimes four jobs at one time because there was nothing to do at home as she was living on her own. During those first two years she managed to save £6000 from her low paid jobs. This was on top of sending regular economic remittances back to her mother, her husband and children, and sometimes her in-laws, in Zimbabwe.

> I was getting a lot of money but I was putting every God given hour into it, into work. Because this full time job that I had, I actually went onto nights after a year. I went over to nights because you did three nights in succession and then you were off for six nights because there were three of us ... So those six days I would maybe sleep the first day and the next five days I would be working different places. Yeah, so I almost like had another full time job outside that other full time job ... I did a bit of cleaning. Like if I was doing my nights I would come back at about half past 8 to do cleaning from 9am to 1pm, then take another shift 8pm to 2am and then go back to my night ... I mean the fact that you knew that you were saving for your children to come and, you know, not want for anything and all that. The thing was the motivator I think.

> You almost felt guilty if you went home to sleep. What am I doing sleeping? I could be out there making some money! It's a good thing I never really fell ill; somehow my body can manage to sustain all that stress for some reason ... And catering was very stressful because we did weddings, they are very social functions and we are so far away from home and some family enjoying themselves and you are on your feet for like 10 hours. So yeah that was the main reason why I gave that up ... They were very social gatherings, for the people it was OK because it was a bit of money because you were doing like 12 or 13 hours, but for me the stress of being there and watching other people enjoying themselves, really families, and I was just on my own. It was just too much ... I was really alone, yeah in the literal sense of being on my own.

On the other hand, Patricia enjoyed care work and particularly liked working with elderly patients. It gave her an opportunity to take responsibility and care for other people and went someway to filling the void left by the separation from her children. Caring appears in her narrative as a central feature in her identity work. Her narrative did not reflect on any stigma attached to care work, as found in other studies of the Zimbabwean community in Britain (McGregor, 2007). Instead it seemed to reinforce her Zimbabwean cultural values of families caring for their own elderly rather than placing them in a home, and it confirmed her sense of herself as a carer and someone who has moral worth.

> LM: What is it that you like about the care work?
>
> P: The care work? I think maybe having been a teacher you want people to kind of appreciate what you are doing or maybe kind of be needed in a way. If you are a parent as well you are used to being needed, you are used to caring. So that need, that kind of deficit that you are, kind of, you know, feeling, you know, you just feel, well you go home and think 'well I think I did a good job today'. It was kind of really the fulfilling bit really.

Skeggs (1997) notes how the 'caring self' is closely linked with discourses of femininity and motherhood. It is both a performance and a technique which enables women to prove themselves as responsible and respectable (1997:69). For Patricia, working in care homes was a means of constructing a caring self and gaining external validation and respectability. By continuing her caring identity across space she was able to assert some moral authority and claim legitimation for her caring capital despite employment which might, on the surface, appear to be demeaning for someone from her background.

As agency staff, her position was precarious and she was dependent on her ability to do the tasks she was asked to do. However, this was difficult as she had no previous experience of domestic work or care homes. She felt vulnerable because she knew that if she made mistakes or asked too many questions this would be fed back to the agency and she wouldn't get further work. She felt she had to present a confident image that suggested that she knew what she was doing. She dreaded being asked about where she'd worked previously as she had to lie. There was no formal training provided at any of the care homes or catering venues she was employed at. Learning was entirely on the job and through social interaction with other staff and patients.

> So you just look at other people and do what they're doing. That is how, because, I had absolutely no idea, like, when these agencies sent me to places I had never been before, I had never been to a place like that and I didn't even know where the wheelchair brakes were [laughing]. Oh my goodness, yeah but because you are not employed there that was actually the way I learnt because you just went there maybe once and, you know, make a few mistakes here and there but you learn and then the next shift you are more confident. I had no, absolutely no idea. [I had] never seen a pad in my life, never seen anything, a commode, in my life and this agency, they didn't ask about your experience, they needed people so much that they just took you. You say 'I want to try' and well they just send you there and then you do whatever.
>
> So it was just like learning from, I mean even the catering jobs, I had never done that but it is something that you just hold a tray and just follow the next person in front of you and ... But I think with the catering, the lady that I used to share a flat with kind of explained to me, you know, the way that you put your plates or which side you are approaching the table and all that. So I had a bit of coaching before I went for that job because ... but it is not like something that you practise at home, you just, when you go you don't want to be the first person out. You want to be the last person so that you can observe the others [laughing]. Yeah, oh yeah, it was a sort of learning curve really. You would have fun sometimes, giggling about a few things here and there and maybe go home and cry about what you would do. Cry 'Oh my God what am I doing with myself?
>
> Now, now I am a senior carer ... Well not officially but I am senior enough to know what I am doing. There are very few things that I don't know, that I haven't met before and because you know it can be a new thing and you are confident enough to ask now, you don't just want to look or maybe make a mistake so you can always ask: Oh I have never done this before, you know, how do I do that? ... Yeah, it is OK [now] not to know, it is OK to say you don't know, you know? You can't know everything. But when you are starting you think: 'Oh, I don't know this'. There is too much that you don't know so you don't want people to know that you don't know that much. Yeah. I mean your life depends on it, that is where your rent is going to come from so if you make a mistake and you lose your job so then what? You try a bit too hard I suppose.

Patricia's identity in the workplace was not singular or static. She was both worker and learner, what Chappell *et al* (2003) refer to as a hybrid worker-learner identity, with learning embedded in the relations with her fellow workers or in some cases with the patients themselves. It was a risky and insecure identity which she constantly feared would be exposed. Her description of learning on the job underlines the essentially social character of learning, and how learning occurs through participating in communities of practice (Lave and Wenger, 1991). As newcomers become more skilled and knowledgeable they move centripetally towards full participation and become old timers, or what Patricia refers to as becoming a 'senior care worker'. As suggested in chapter three, the centripetal movement in the community of practice to full membership and competence involves a shift in identity (Lave and Wenger, 1991; Wenger, 1998). For Patricia, her identity becomes one of competent care worker, capable and confident enough to ask questions where necessary rather than having to lie to cover up her lack of experience and knowledge. To paraphrase Wenger, and viewing identity as a form of competence, she has moved into 'familiar territory' where what was 'foreign', 'opaque', 'unwieldy' and 'unproductive', becomes 'familiar', 'understandable', 'usable' and 'negotiable' (1998:153).

A consequence of this shift is that Patricia's sense of self is transformed, not only in relation to her ability to do the job, but also in relation to her fellow workers. As we see later, this new sense of social confidence meant that she was no longer prepared to endure the low expectations and racial prejudice of some of her fellow care workers. She was able to start negotiating a new identity, which ultimately would lead her back into formal education. First I want to pick up the story of Patricia as a mother.

It took much longer than expected for her children to get permission to come to the UK. Being separated from her children for such a long time was difficult and painful for Patricia. As noted, caring is a significant and constant theme in her identity and being separated conflicted with this identity.

> I mean initially they said it was going to be a year. I thought well a year is reasonable, you know, you miss one Christmas, you miss one birthday, its reasonable; and then you miss a second birthday, you miss a second Christmas, you know it wasn't.

Festivals and holidays were particularly difficult times and underlined her sense of isolation and loneliness. Even in care work she would be reminded of her family.

> Christmases, even these care jobs, Christmases and like families would come in and be with their residents and you know, it was still difficult for me because I was one person who didn't have anything to do on such days like Christmas and all that. So I was one person who was available to work on such days, you know, you are there, you know, and it is double time as well, you know. Yeah, so and sometimes I would, like, one of the places that I worked was run by this couple so I had to ask for the phone and go upstairs and phone my children, wish them a happy Christmas from there. Oh yeah and then go downstairs and see other families together and all that. Yeah, it was quite difficult, it was very difficult. You never really, it was difficult for me to get used to it, you know? I mean, like we are a very social culture, very sociable. So you don't really spend a Christmas by, just you and your children, your husband, your children, it's like maybe three families together. So after all that time and, you just sort of want to go home.

As time went on she found it more and more difficult to explain to the children why they weren't able to join her or why she couldn't come back to them. She began to fear that they were beginning to see her less as a mother, with a maternal, caring role and more as someone who just provided them with material goods.

> ... after about a year, 18 months I think, they would then start asking for things. That is why I wanted them to come here before their dad because they were asking for things, you almost feel like you are not, that maternal thing is not there anymore, you are just providing things that they want and they just look at you as somebody who provides things that they want, you know? ... So it was really, you feel like you are losing that connection that maternal bond. I deliberately kind of wanted him [her husband] to stay behind for a couple of months because the children, I wanted some kind of bond with the children on my own kind of thing.

Patricia had saved up enough money so that she wouldn't have to work for the first three or four months after the children arrived. She wanted to be able to spend time re-establishing her relationship with them. Although obviously overjoyed to be reunited with her children, being a parent in the UK brought new and unexpected challenges, as she was forced into new and unfamiliar roles and the family had to adapt to their reduced circumstances in the UK.

> What was that like? Oh it was terrible! The first experience was really terrible because I was living in a bed-sit and that was home for me and then there they were. 'Let's go upstairs, let's go home!' And it was just one room; it was one room with a bed there and a stove there. 'So is this where we are going to live?' I think that actually it was maybe terrible for me more than for them.

Eventually after spending a few weeks in bed and breakfast accommodation, the family were re-housed in more appropriate accommodation.

Patricia's narrative (like Maryam's in chapter four) highlights the learning processes and role shifts involved in parenting in a new social space. She describes her biggest challenge and steepest learning curve in the UK as being when her children joined her and she was expected to run her own home and care for them. Accustomed to domestic help and living in a school compound, she struggled to manage the gendered tensions between her role as caretaker and mother, and the role of breadwinner. The parental involvement in children's lives in the UK was strange and having her children here highlighted aspects of UK culture she had been unaware of before.

> Taking the children to school it was almost like a job. First thing in the morning you take them to school and then before you know it you are going to pick them up. You think 'My goodness is this going to end at all?' It was really hard. In Zimbabwe the children don't have to walk any distances and there are no dangers really that you expect them to encounter on the way home. They never experienced living away from school; it was always within the school fence. So you never really worried about children travelling ... Here you don't know your neighbour well enough to trust them to let your child just go in and out of someone else's house. You can't do that. When I was on my own I didn't really notice how people socialised, because it was just me. I'd met my friends at the places where I worked and I didn't realise it was different when you had children.
>
> [In Zimbabwe] someone washes for them and somebody does everything for them. You're just there as a mum, you know, to sort out this and this problem ... Here it is much harder work, much, much harder. There is so much that you have to do, so much, and so little space. I feel I'm confined here and I'm not used to that very small space. I'm not used to having my children within ten metres of me all the time. In houses, even outdoors ... I feel I'm becoming a bit controlling of them because they're there on the

> computer and you say 'I think you've been there too long', they're watching TV and you say 'I think you've been ...' they're playing on the X-box and you say 'Do your homework'. I feel like I'm controlling the kids now because that's all they do, either they're on the X-box, or the Play Station or the TV – that's how they play – and I think 'Oh no, stop this, stop this'. You feel like really, really controlling ... [In Zimbabwe] they'd be playing outdoors, with some neighbours that you know, maybe the next-door neighbours.

Her husband arrived four months later. This did not make things easier as it took him longer than expected to get a job, putting an additional strain on family relations.

> So it wasn't what we expected because in terms of, er, even the quality of living. You can imagine – I had two maids at some stages. You don't do any washing up; you don't do any mopping, washing or ironing. You just go to school, you just tell your maid what you want for lunch, you go to school, you come home, have your lunch, you go back, leave her to do the dishes. You come home, have your supper and you go to bed. So, here you are thinking that you are making a lot of money and then you see that you are doing everything yourself ... It was okay when I was on my own, I mean I didn't really need to do that much of ironing or washing-up or cooking. Because if you eat at work you don't really need to come in and prepare something. You just have a sandwich and go to bed. But then when my children came, I thought 'My goodness, I am the maid and I am the bread-winner. I am the maid, I am doing everything!' It was a shock, because I've never done it in all my life.

The difficulty Patricia experienced trying to gain a placement in a school and her sense of the poor discipline in UK schools had persuaded her not to re-train as a teacher. Instead she decided that once her family was reunited and settled that she would return to study and qualify as a mental health nurse. She felt this would provide a route into caring in a professional capacity with more remuneration and higher status. Assuming the identity of learner was also a way of overcoming racial prejudice and the low expectations of her held by the other care workers. She describes agency work as an environment where people 'tend to take advantage of other people'. She felt that it was not necessarily, or always, on grounds of race, but could also be because of being new in a place, unlike the permanent staff. As agency staff you were treated with less respect and given the worst jobs to do. This echoes McGregor's findings of the 'friction' between temporary staff who are predominantly African or other migrants, and the predominantly white permanent staff (McGregor, 2007). However, institutionalised racism and the low expectations the other care workers had of her as a Black African were significant in motivating her to return to study. Race was one of the pivotal markers of her habitus in the field of care work and clearly signalled her inferior position in that field. To negotiate her way out of this reduced position Patricia was able to mobilise the educational capital accumulated in the predominantly white and middle class boarding school in Zimbabwe. Returning to education was a way of transforming her identity, proving her abilities and respectability.

> When you go into workplaces because not only are you African but you are also Black, people don't expect you to, to have any kind of education. So you are always out to prove yourself which is really what motivated me into [mental health nursing]. There was a time when I was comfortable with my care jobs, earning enough to send home and look after myself. But then I thought, every place you go you have to prove yourself and you can always take out your certificates and say 'Well, I've got O-levels, I've got a teaching diploma, I've got A-levels'. You can always do that. It's really stressful to always try to say 'I'm not what you expect or what you think', so the only way was to be in education yourself to be professional and then people don't question you. They don't question your ability because they know you're going through the education process. Because it's really difficult out there when you go to places and even the basic things people think you don't know that or they ask 'Are there things like this in Zimbabwe?' Or 'Can you write the simple reports for what happened to the residents?' and you think 'Yes: I can write! I can spell!' It is that you have to prove yourself. If you're doing a care job where you don't need any qualifications how are you proving yourself? That is one thing I realised.

She describes how when her fellow care workers treated her as if she didn't know anything, she would 'pull out that nurse training course card'. Being a student and returning to education, even though in a different country, was an enjoyable and straightforward process for her. The ability to convert her educational capital to symbolic capital brought with it a sense of confidence, security and entitlement enabling the production and reformation of identity:

> I didn't really doubt my academic ability because that is what I am, I am an academic, I like the reading, the essays, the exams, all that. ... I like the enrichment of being on the receiving end ...

Patricia managed to pay her course fees and combine her full time study with working and supporting her family. Her experiences in higher education are picked up in chapter ten. Patricia has graduated and is continuing care work while looking for employment as a mental health nurse.

In both Patricia's and Maryam's narratives we see how the central axis in their lives shifts in response to their caring responsibilities. In Patricia's case, we see how her focus and main identity shifts from worker and money earner, to caring for her children and struggling to re-establishing her identity as a mother in a culture with very different norms and expectations. Once her children were settled she draws on the capital of her bourgeoise and, importantly, British education to return to a viable and confident identity of her past: that of student and a person working towards qualifications. Eventually, she achieves the professional identity of mental health nurse.

6

Farideh: the Iranian nutritionalist's story

When we met, Farideh had been in the UK for four years. During the time I've known her she has experienced significant personal difficulties and upheavals. After divorcing her husband, she endured isolation from the Iranian community in which she was living. Weaving through Farideh's story is an unhappiness with, and resistance to, the traditional gender identities and ascriptions of the Iranian Islamic Republic. The curtailment of her dress, her choice of study and employment, and especially gender oppression are threaded throughout her narrative. Migration offered a new social space which opened up alternative possibilities and gender positions, including living on her own as an independent woman.

Farideh is an intensely private person, preferring not to discuss her personal life in the context of this research. Much of our interview time was taken up with discussions about her formal learning experiences and is reflected in the narrative presented here. Her narrative highlights the struggle to adapt to the very different expectations of the UK higher education system and to establish a positive learner identity for herself when the value of her capital has been measured and fixed as being of little worth in the UK.

Life in Iran

Farideh was born in Shiraz in southern Iran in the late 1950s. Her father was a lawyer, until he was prevented from practising under the Shah's regime. Amidst growing discontent and opposition to the Shah in the 1970s, he set up a newspaper, but that too was shut down as it was perceived to be anti-establishment. She describes herself as having been a studious child who loved school. She worked hard and achieved high grades throughout her primary and high school. Towards the end of high school she became increasingly politicised and was particularly moved by the plight of the Palestinian people. She began to read books about Islam and politics written in Persian by Marxist and Iranian oppositionists, books which under the Shah's regime were banned. In her final year of high school she didn't achieve good grades and she ascribes this to her political activity.

The Iranian Revolution occurred in 1979, the year Farideh left high school. Almost immediately, the new regime introduced a raft of restrictive measures against women. These included changes in family law which clearly disadvantaged women, forced *hejab* (long dress and headscarf), and restrictions on women's choice of work (Sanasarian, 1992). Farideh laughs as she tells me about the Western-style clothing and very short skirts she used to wear at high school. During the early days of the revolution she had to wear a black *chador*, the outer garment worn in public to cover a woman from head to ankles, but later this was relaxed to the *hejab*. She describes how she felt suffocated in the headscarf and how she couldn't hear or think well when she wore it; even when in the fresh air she felt stifled. The long dress didn't bother her too much but she would remove the headscarf at every opportunity. Institutional cleansing or *paak saazi* barred women from entering Government institutions if they were wearing make-up, had a manicure or any hair showing (Honarbin-Holliday, 2008).

Farideh applied to university and started a degree in veterinary science in the north of Iran. However, a year and a half into the degree the Islamic Cultural Revolution took place and all the universities were shut for three years while a new academic cadre and national curriculum was put in place. One of the changes was that some subjects were deemed unsuitable for girls and women, for example agriculture or geology, because they required exposure to the outside/public sphere. Laboratory sciences, midwifery and nursing were considered better suited to women's nature, confined as they were to the inside/private arena, and in the case of midwifery and nursing placed women in largely all female environments (Sanasarian, 1992). Consequently Farideh was unable to continue with veterinary science and three years later started a second degree in nutritional science. So in the space of just a few years Farideh had to negotiate her way through the changed religious and cultural norms brought about by the Cultural Revolution. This was most visibly represented in the prohibition ofWestern clothing and the introduction of an Islamic dress code, but also in the behaviour, areas of study and employment assigned to women. A dramatically changed gender ideology began to map out and constrain women's agency.

It was a difficult time when her brother, a doctor, and her younger sister, who was just fourteen, were arrested. Both were accused of supporting the *Mojahedin*, a left wing political group, who were prominent in the movement against the Shah. Her brother was imprisoned in Shiraz, and her sister in Tehran. Although the *Mojahedin* had played an important part in bringing the Ayatollah Khomeini to power they subsequently became the main opposition to his Islamic Republic and faced brutal persecution. Between 1981 and 1988 over six thousand *Mojahedin* were executed (Abrahamian, 1992).

Farideh describes how, as both her parents were distressed and unwell, much of the prison visiting fell to her. She would make the long journey by bus back to Shiraz twice a week, carrying her books and a small torch so she could study on the journey. Despite these emotional upheavals in her family life, she graduated with good grades and did a one-year mandatory placement for the government, overseeing quality control in a food science laboratory. She describes this as the best time in her life; it was her first taste of paid employment and of real independence. She had three proposals of marriage in one year, all of which she refused. Once she had finished her placement she returned to live with her parents, but found it difficult to find work. She describes how at interviews she wasn't asked about her experience for the job or why she was applying; instead she was asked questions about Islam and her observation and understanding of religious practices. When she failed these questions she was told to go away and study religious texts.

She eventually got a job managing a residential unit for female students, but quickly found the requirement to give preferential treatment to certain groups at odds with her own sense of fairness. She describes the system of allocating accommodation to students as corrupt, with priority given to the families of martyrs – those whose fathers or brothers had been killed in the Iran-Iraq war – rather than allocated according to need. When Farideh wrote a letter to her manager expressing concern at the unfairness she was transferred to a mail sorting office.

Farideh finally got a job working as a nutritionist in a children's hospital. The job was not easy, as it involved supervising seventeen male kitchen staff who did not want a female manager. The first year was characterised by deliberate campaigns to undermine and stymie her attempts to do the job, but eventually she managed to get the workers to accept her and she held the job down for eight years.

During this time Farideh got married to a man who also worked at the hospital. She said she had not wanted to get married, but that in Iran it was by then impossible for a woman in her early thirties not to be married. She 'just wanted to be independent, but I couldn't do that in my country'. Sanasarian (1992) describes how at this time 'marriage was relentlessly advocated by the state' (1992:61). The official marriage age was reduced to thirteen for girls, polygamous and 'temporary' marriages were encouraged, and women's rights to divorce were severely limited. Sanasarian suggests this pressure to marry corresponded to the state's need to reduce the number of unmarried females (and hence control female sexuality), and to increase the birthrate at a time of huge loss of life in the war with Iraq (1980-1988). Despite the Islamic Republic's ideology that the natural and main responsibility for women was motherhood, women were still needed in the workforce. The war had devastated the economy, reduced the male workforce and increased the number of female headed households. However, the state's contradictory gender ideology meant that women's experience in the workforce was often fraught with conflict and struggle (Sanasarian, 1992), as in Farideh's case.

Life in Iran became unbearably difficult for her and for her family as persecution over any opposition to the regime intensified. Her older brother was executed by the government, and so was her younger sister – at the age of sixteen. Her other sister fled to the USA. Farideh and her husband's flight from Iran was terrifying and sudden. She describes how:

> I was doing my job very happily, but something happened and we did something wrong and we had to come here.

Learning and living in the UK

Farideh and her husband arrived in the UK in 2000. She describes being in a very distressed state when she arrived and had no idea even which country she was in; she is still not sure which town they first arrived in. Social Services immediately referred her for medical treatment and she was given permission to delay her application for asylum while she underwent treatment for her mental health. Farideh and her husband eventually applied for, and were granted, refugee status within a year of arriving in the UK. Over the next few years Farideh attended college to improve her English. To support herself she worked as a cleaner, a care assistant, a community worker and for the past four years as a hospitality assistant, preparing and setting out food for meetings and conferences in a local hospital.

When I first met Farideh she was part-way through a Masters degree in clinical nutrition at a higher education institute. She was keen to practice as a nutritionalist in the UK and believed that the Masters degree would put her on the path. I first interviewed her after her first year of a two year Masters. She had been commuting to London twice a week, which was hugely expensive in travelling costs as well as course fees. The distance also contributed to her sense of isolation. She told me:

> It's very interesting and I like it, but I wasn't looking for something interesting, I was looking for something to guide me into work. It's a taught course and I enjoy it a lot and I'm learning new things. But up to now I haven't seen a hospital and really I don't know what a nutritionalist does in the UK. I don't know ... It's a 2 year course and I've finished the first year but I'm not sure about the second year because if I can't gain any experience of work ... I mean I don't need a new certificate ... well I need one but the most important thing for me is to find some way of finding a job. I think there is a high demand for this job and it's very competitive and I'm not optimistic about finding a job.

Farideh found university in the UK confusing and disturbing as she struggled to decipher the unfamiliar academic writing conventions, the learning styles, technicalities of referencing and the expectations of tutors regarding academic assignments.

> It was very difficult for me really and for the first term, because it was the first time that I wanted to study scientific material in English and I didn't know how to start. For the first month or two I used to translate from English to my language and then I read it in my language but then I couldn't express it in English so I couldn't work. I have learnt a lot. It has been a lot of work, a lot, a lot. ... Especially in the first term I didn't know how to write essays. It was the first time. I didn't know I had to reference any of my writing so I had to re-write it ... I had a letter attached to the essay saying there are no references ... They didn't show me how to write them.
>
> They also said that the paragraphs are not friendly [sic]. I didn't know I could use sub-titles in my essay because in the English course I learnt that when I write an article or something I don't have to use sub-titles. Then I read essays from different journals and I compared it with myself and my essay. I used to write at university in Iran, but it was very different. I didn't have to reference everything, I used to write references at the end only, not for all the sentences in the middle of the essay, not in the text.
>
> Also, presentations were very, very, very difficult. The first presentation I didn't know what is a presentation. Eighteen years ago we had presentations in Iran, but we didn't have PowerPoint or overheads. It was very embarrassing the first time. When I wanted to do my presentation I didn't have PowerPoint on my computer [so] I used overhead slides. I was very nervous, I couldn't finish it because I was shaking ... [laughs] ... Yes, I was shaking, my voice was shaking and I couldn't remember where the overhead was, it was on the ceiling and people couldn't see it, but I was very embarrassed. I couldn't look. I couldn't look behind and control it and see where it was, on the board or on the wall. I couldn't finish that first one. But the second one I had experience.
>
> I asked my tutor [if I could] attend presentation of other students in other subjects and courses and it was very helpful. I took notes and then I understood that I had to have introduction and this and this and this. And then the second time I used PowerPoint. It was better; I think I got ... 59 per cent [laughs]. I'd never done presentations like this before! At the same time it was a very difficult time in my life and then I had to study so hard and this added to it.
>
> I felt isolated on the course because I didn't know anyone. I tried to make good communication with other students, [pause] but I wasn't successful and I felt completely isolated. Yes, it was very difficult. I lost 8 kilos. Yes, it

> was from everything. I studied from 6am to 10pm. I had to write, for example, 4,000 words; it was the first time I wrote a review.
>
> There was an option course in Health Science which I wanted to do. When I read the paper it was written that it was in Autumn and Spring; so I though I'd do it in the Spring. When I went to start the course it had started in September and I didn't have chance to go to the class to learn how to write a review. I had to do the whole course in just two months. I had two 15 minute meetings with my tutor and then I used the computer to try and find out how to write a review. I had almost written 4000 words when I showed it to my tutor; she took away 3000 words. She said that you don't have to write a lot of information about the topic that you want to present. ... So I started to write it again. I started again. It was very difficult, but I finished it. I'm waiting for the result now.

Lillis (2001) speaks of an 'institutional practice of mystery' to describe how higher education fails to make explicit or teach the conventions of the literacy practice it demands. Lea and Street (1998) argue that, far from being monolithic or transparent, literacy practices vary across disciplines, courses and tutors, and that such variations are at the level of 'epistemology, authority and contestation over knowledge', rather than skills or competences (1998:160). They argue that it is not valid to claim that such concepts are generic or transferable or that they represent 'common sense ways of knowing'. Lillis (2001) argues that 'essayist' literacy practices represent a particular way of knowing and being which: 'privileges the discursive routines of particular social groups whilst dismissing those of people who, culturally and communally, have access to and engage in a range of other practices' (Lillis, 2001:39).

Farideh's habitus and social background rendered her confused and an outsider in the UK higher education field. She did not have access to the cultural and social capital which could help her make informed choices about whether the Masters programme was appropriate for her employment goals. Instead she relied on the 'cold knowledge' provided by the college rather than the 'hot knowledge' available through social networks or inherited knowledge (Ball *et al*, 2000). She didn't have the cultural capital to help her to read and understand the academic timetable or to decipher the expectations and conventions of academic practices. To use Bourdieu's (1992) analogy of the game, she didn't know the written and unwritten rules and what the most effective strategies might be to ensure academic success.

The cultural capital that had taken her so long to acquire in Iran was fixed as being inferior and lacking in value. Aware of this evaluation, Farideh had a sense of herself as an inferior student, and this contributed to her feelings of insecurity and anxiety in higher education. She didn't have the confidence or cultural understanding that it was acceptable to ask questions, or establish a dialogue with her tutors at an early stage, which could have rendered her experience less difficult and traumatic.

Despite her proficiency in English, Farideh worried about making mistakes in her written work and not being able to understand everything that went on in the classroom. She'd been unable to locate any support services at the university which might have been able to help her.

> When I finished my essays I didn't know how to correct my English mistakes and I couldn't find anything in the university because as I said I used to go just two days. I found someone to help me at the college. I paid £80. I gave her £80 to look at two essays and correct my English. However, when I had my results it said that I mixed UK and American English [laughs].
>
> I had a bit of difficulty in that course and the other people had a very high level of English so I had to listen very, very carefully to understand and sometimes I couldn't. I wanted to buy a tape recorder but you know the course was very expensive and I had to pay for everything. My travel was expensive, sometimes I had to pay £40 for the train because I had to be there at 9am. It was very, very expensive. I had a little bit of savings but I spent them all this first year ... I applied for a loan from the bank, but who trusts a refugee who doesn't have any job and any money in their account?

Farideh never did return after the first year to complete her Masters degree and exited with a diploma. It was a difficult time in her personal life as she was in the process of separating from and divorcing her husband. This involved moving away, both physically and emotionally, from the Iranian community in which she had been living. It was at this point that she started the WILAW course, in search of a new and different direction which would provide greater opportunities for employment in the UK. She decided to study pharmacy, as she felt this was most likely to lead to employment and also would enable her to work in hospitals. She was accepted on an undergraduate degree course as long as she brushed up her knowledge of chemistry, which she did by taking an A Level in chemistry.

Farideh is enjoying the pharmacy course, although she still struggles with the differences in the education systems, learning styles and expectations. She describes how lecturers in Iran used to give them all they needed to learn, so that when they left the lecture they knew what they needed to know and what they had to do:

> In my country, lecturers, they work much harder than students to give the students what they need to know. I don't want to say it's good, but it's easy for students because they have everything ready, just they read and they learn it. But here they just show the way, give you one sentence and you have to go and find from the books and you can't find it in one book. So it's very time consuming and I'm very slow in reading, so it took me a lot of time ...

Lacking explicit guidance on what texts to read was difficult. Farideh described the time it took her to search for information and then to identify what was relevant to her purposes. She described the time spent looking for books and information as 'wasted time' which could have been spent studying. When we met during her second year of studies, she talked about the lack of books and how she felt she was not getting the feedback she needed to improve her work. She was also finding the volume of work difficult to manage alongside her paid employment. Despite all these difficulties, she talked of 'loving' studying and how lucky she was to have that opportunity.

Since Farideh had been in the UK, her father has died, leaving just her mother and a younger sister in Iran. She phones her mother every Tuesday and her sister in the USA every Saturday. She talks in a matter of fact manner about her parents' generation, many of whom are left in Iran and have lost their children in the wars or from executions or through migration.

She likes living in the UK but feels there is 'always something missing'. Although she has been here for eight years she still feels she doesn't belong here:

> As a refugee I felt you are living somewhere that you don't belong to. Especially English people; they are not very interested with communicating with ... I can't say foreign people, it's asylum seekers. What can I say ... there is not a good perception of refugees, the view is not good of refugees. Maybe there is a definition of refugees as people who come to this country for

> benefits and unfortunately the very, very little cases it's true, but we can't expand it to everyone. When I speak to English people the first question they ask me is 'When do you intend to go back?' What can I say? I think English people trust the media. It affects people.

However, she doesn't believe the situation for women is getting any better in Iran and believes it would be very difficult for a woman on her own to live and work there. She says she would love to go back to live, and believes that one day she will, perhaps '... after I'm 65, when I'm an old woman and can just live'.

The political situation in Iran took a sudden and unexpected turn in June 2009 with the announcement of the Iranian presidential election results. When President Mahmoud Ahmadinejad was returned with a large majority, supporters of the opposition leader Mir Hussein Mousavi and his 'Green Revolution' took to the streets. Such mass demonstrations as occurred in major cities across the country had not been seen since the overthrow of the Shah in 1979. Farideh and I met while the demonstrations were going on and she described herself as excited and scared in equal measure. She was excited at the possibility of change, but scared for the young people demonstrating and what the regime could do to them; she recalled the loss of her brother and sister and what this had meant to her family. Despite her caution, the events had clearly changed how she felt about Iran and the possibilities for her future. For the first time she could imagine the possibility of returning, either for a visit or perhaps to live, but she would wait and see what happened.

7

Savalan: the Iranian entrepreneur's story

Savalan is the youngest of the participants in this research. He arrived in the UK in 2004 at the age of twenty-four. The narrative presented here describes his first five years in the UK and his determined efforts to learn to speak English perfectly and to understand the new culture in which he found himself. He demonstrates a strategic approach to the transition process: consciously making decisions that will enhance his language learning, support the development of networks with non-refugees and enable him to re-gain the status and economic position he enjoyed in Iran. This sense of agency is also illustrated in his decision to change his name to something which more accurately reflects his cultural and ethnic background. His narrative draws attention to the significance of transnational relationships with family members left behind, and the complexities involved in trying to reconcile different aspects of his identity. It also highlights the vulnerability and anxiety created by the impact on him of the Government's policy of giving refugees temporary right to remain in the UK for just five years.

Life in Iran

Savalan was born in Azerbaijan in north-west Iran in 1980 and grew up during the first decade of the Iranian Cultural Revolution. Under the Shah's regime his father had worked in personal security in Iran, but after the revolution in 1979 the family fled to Azerbaijan to escape the reprisals against people who had worked for the regime. Once in Azerbaijan his father set up his own business. Savalan describes Azerbaijan as being completely separate from Iran, with its own language and culture.

His parents had five daughters before finally having a son, which he says meant that he was considered the most important child and he lived a 'protected life'. His parents indulged him and gave him most of their affections and attention. He didn't particularly enjoy school and describes the teachers as too strict. It was during the war with Iraq and he explained how the government's encouragement for families to have more children meant that classrooms were often overcrowded and some schools had two or three shifts a day to accommodate all of the children; there was also pressure from his parents to study hard and do well at school, and any failure was punished. His happiest memories were of the summer holidays when he would go to stay with his grandparents on a small farm in the countryside. He remembers enjoying being a teenager, spending time with his three best friends, free from responsibilities. He said he was alienated from the Iranian regime and was critical of the restrictions on behaviour, clothing and hairstyles they imposed upon teenagers. He'd always been interested in politics; discussing and debating political issues was part of his family life. There was no access to the internet when he was growing up, but they would listen to BBC Farsi which was broadcast from abroad. The Government would try to disrupt the frequency and they would constantly have to re-tune the radio to try and pick it up.

Savalan left secondary education with a diploma in maths and physics. He began studying to take the entrance exam for university but felt that in Iran at that time there was no guarantee of a well-paid job after university. He describes university in Iran as 'a waste of time' for his generation, as graduate unemployment was so high. In the late 1990s, even as relations with some foreign Governments began to thaw, the economy still suffered from low investment and high unemployment. The Cultural Revolution had weakened Iran's science and technology and the economy was overwhelmingly dependent on oil. Both male and female graduates were (and still are) facing high levels of unemployment and finding suitable employment remains a major problem (Keddie, 2006).

When an opportunity arose for Savalan to train in ICT he took it, believing that as this was a relatively new and growing field in Iran he would fare better as an entrepreneur in commerce than if he studied for four years only to face poor employment prospects. His mother sold some jewellery to buy him a computer and he went to Tehran to study. After training, Savalan worked for a year in a company assembling, repairing and selling computers, before setting up his own business. In just four years he had a profitable business, his own flat and a very comfortable life in Iran.

Savalan told me that he had broken Sharia law in Iran, but that it concerned 'a fundamental freedom and [was] not against the law in other countries'. When he discovered that his life was in danger, he sold some of the business to raise money for his escape. He describes how he paid a lot of money which made the journey relatively short, just two weeks as opposed to the months it can take people who come overland. He had only confided in one sister that he was leaving, the rest of his family and friends he contacted by phone once he was safely out of Iran. Savalan was fairly matter of fact about leaving the business he had built up:

> I lost what I had done for five years. And then in one go [clicks his fingers] you lose everything. But I am happy here, and I am safe.

It was his family, especially his mother, who he felt most sad about leaving.

Learning and living in the UK

When Savalan arrived he was sent to a hotel in Dover where he stayed for forty five days with two hundred other Iranians. It was an unpleasant experience. He describes how the high concentration of asylum seekers in the town had fostered hostile feelings towards refugees and asylum seekers among the local population. It was Christmas time and they were curious to see how English people celebrated the festive season, but after one of them was physically attacked, they didn't go out much, especially in the evenings. Instead they watched the Christmas celebrations on television. He made friends with the manager of the hotel, who taught him basic rules of etiquette and how to greet people. She also taught him the importance of saying 'thank you' and 'please' at the appropriate times, and he frequently went to her for help in understanding and deciphering the new culture.

His expectations of the UK had been shaped by television in Iran and he relates how he had expected everyone to be walking the streets carrying lap tops and guns. It was not as he had expected it to be and he talked at length about the differences between the two cultures: food, tea drinking, the political openness in the UK, the pubs and bars, the focus on the nuclear family rather than extended family and friends, and the 'English reserve'. He talks of the culture shock he experienced on arrival:

> Everything was numb. For forty five days I was numb in Dover, I didn't fear because I was like shocked. I couldn't see properly what was going on ...You see the boxers they box, one of them punch and they can't see. You are shocked. I was like that ... coming here and, you know, facing gay people! We haven't got gay people, we haven't got lesbians. Like I saw two men kissing each other and I was like, 'What's going on here?' But it was very interesting, you go somewhere and you face something that you never experienced so, yeh.
>
> LM: So what did you think about that, when you saw these shocking things?
>
> S: Just, first it was interesting, then second I was happy that I am seeing a new thing ... I have a chance to see what's going on in Western country, and how people think in the West. And another thing I always respect them. ... If I don't respect you, you won't respect me. So respect any new ideas, however I found them, they may be silly or stupid in my mind first time but I said 'Okay it is their belief, I need to respect them'.

He feels people are lonelier and more depressed here in the UK. He was shocked at how many people he saw sitting alone watching television when he walked home at night. He found this sad and felt that both cultures had something to offer – you just had to try and pick the best bits from each.

After the forty five days Savalan and nine other Iranians were dispersed to accommodation around the country while his case was processed by the Home Office. He talks of his life at this point as being in three sections: his case with the Home Office, learning English and his private life. It was a time of considerable vulnerability and anxiety: letters from the Home Office and from his solicitor were all in English and he didn't know anyone who spoke English well enough to translate for him. He would take the letters to Migrant Helpline (a charity, partly funded by the UK Home Office, providing assistance and support for asylum seekers and refugees) and hope that a translator could be found quickly, otherwise there were delays in finding out what was happening with his case. He feels that the difficulty and delays that language posed was an issue in many of the rejected cases for asylum: people didn't always know what was going on in their cases and didn't have time to respond.

He enrolled on an English language course at a local college and worked hard to learn and improve his English (until 2007 asylum seekers were entitled to attend government funded ESOL classes). He was scornful of the English language teaching he had received in Iran; the teachers had never been to the UK so much of the pronunciation and expressions he had learnt were incorrect. He describes having very little English language when he arrived and having to mime to express himself. Learning English was a priority for him, not only in the functional sense of wanting to be able to communicate and express himself, but also because becoming a competent speaker was closely linked to his sense of identity and self-esteem.

> And I remember that I didn't go out at night or whatever, I just stayed home, watching telly and any single new word that I came across, I checked it in the dictionary. How they say it, how they speak, because I realised that speaking English language is essential for me even much more than getting refugee status. ... There were some circumstances that I couldn't say what I wanted, and people thought that I am stupid, because I can't talk. So I wanted to prove to them, No, I am not able to speak English language doesn't mean that I don't know or I am stupid.

He moved to a different college the following autumn in order to be with a broader range of students. He was the only refugee or asylum seeker in the class.

> You mix up with other students who are not refugees, so you can learn with them more, and socialise with them. So I went to register my name at [name] College, I took an exam and it was September 2005 I was still an asylum seeker and I went and I was very, very lucky that I had a very, very kind teacher, she is a friend now.

Because he sometimes had to miss classes to go to the Home Office, he told the teacher that he was an asylum seeker. But he didn't tell any of the students. Even when he received the phone call from his solicitor during one of his English classes confirming that he had been granted refugee status he still didn't reveal his identity to his fellow students. He had been in the UK for almost a year when he received his status and he describes how he stood weeping with relief outside the classroom as he tried to phone his mother in Iran to tell her.

But Savalan had only been granted refugee status for five years. In our early interviews he did not appear too concerned about this temporary status; he was just keen to start his life here in the UK without fearing the prospect of imminent deportation back to Iran. For Savalan, getting refugee status meant he could now plan what he was going to do with his life. He knew that competition in the ICT field would make it impossible for him to establish and succeed in business in the way he had done in Iran, and that the best chance he had of working in business was to go to university and study for a degree. He took a one year Access to Business course before taking the Ways into Learning and Work course and applying for a degree. This gave him the opportunity to continue improving his English language and to develop the academic language, skills and conventions needed to succeed in HE.

On the Access course, he was studying with English students for the first time. He found this frightening at first because he still felt embarrassed by his English. However, the practical experience, ideas and understanding he'd built up in Iran through running his own business gave him confidence. He was able to make links with some of the theoretical ideas and realised that in many ways he had an edge on the other students. The frustration of not being able to express his ideas further encouraged him to work harder at his English language studies. He continued to make lists of new vocabulary 'then I practise, practise, practise them'. Again he didn't tell any of the other students that he was a refugee.

> I think it was a big worry if people asked me 'what are you doing here?'. What can I say because, like I am a refugee but I have got respect for myself, I don't want to be down in front of people. Okay so you know, all of them are free here they can, you know, but I am a refugee. So I didn't like this idea of telling people I am a refugee. First, I thought it was so personal, that to tell them I was a refugee was my personal life. And the other thing is I thought this may affect me badly, if I tell them it would put me down, like bring my morale down, you know, and I don't like people being sympathetic to me all the time. 'Yeh, you know, he's a refugee,' or something, I don't like that and the other thing is that it is embarrassing really. Em-

> barrassing that I come from, I don't know, come from a bad country you know. So I prefer not telling them why I am here and what for. I just always say at the beginning that I am a student.

Savalan went on to explain that just as in Iran, British people are affected by what the Government says. He finds this surprising in light of the freedom of the press and widespread access to the internet. He blames the British Government and the media for the negative and hostile perception of refugees.

> They never say this refugee did something good. Everything what they say about refugees is bad. Okay, but they don't want to say Savalan came here three years ago he hasn't got a criminal record, he has never fought, he's in education and you know he hasn't got any problems and he is refugee so we can have a refugee without any problem, and if we keep them in the future they will be very good for our society you know. They never say that, you know what I mean?

It was at this time that Savalan decided to change his name. He was named Abdullah, after his great grandfather. It was a name he hadn't liked much in Iran, but he'd put up with it as it was a very common name and he felt it was somehow normal. He said it was not possible to change your name in Iran so he had not thought of it as an option. However, in the UK he began to question why he had an Arabic name rather than an Azari or Farsi name, which he felt would indicate his ethnicity, his background and culture.

> When I arrived here I realised it more and more that the name that I have I don't like it. It has nothing to do with my culture and my background.

He resented people making the wrong assumptions about his identity and assuming that he was Arabic. He chose the name Savalan after an Azerbaijani political singer/songwriter who sings about an autonomous, independent Azerbaijan. It is also the name of a landmark near his hometown, Ardabil. So the name signified his minority identity in both the UK and Iran.

Savalan successfully completed the Access course and after the WILAW course progressed straight onto a Batchelor's degree in international business. It is a four-year sandwich course with the opportunity to spend one year in another country, and he'd already applied to go to the USA for a year. He was concerned because his five years leave to remain would expire the year before he was due to graduate. Although he says he was trying not to think about it, it became a recurrent topic in our later interviews. We frequently discussed what made a 'good British citizen' and what criteria the Home Office might draw upon when assessing whether he could stay in the UK or whether he would be returned to Iran.

> I was one of the first group of refugees to get five years. We don't know what will happen, we have to wait and then apply for British citizenship and see what happens. I believe they are going to look at what we've done during this time, any criminal records or did we pay tax? What have we done during this four or five years, can we speak English? I think they will look at these things. There are some refugees who've been here a long time, but they don't speak English and they need translators and I think the government doesn't want such citizens and I think that's fair enough. I think the government is going to look at our performance, what we've done.

He went on to talk about the cost of educating him and how 'stupid' it would be to send him back just when society could begin to reap the benefits of his education. In the end, because of his fear that he might be deported, Savalan decided against going to the USA for a year and instead completed his degree in three years. At least that way he has completed his degree and has a UK qualification before his visa expires. His plan was to try and find employment immediately on completion. But this proved impossible because he only had five months left on his visa when he graduated. This, he acknowledged, made it difficult to convince an employer that he was suitable for graduate employment. Savalan therefore faced a further period of waiting and insecurity until he applied for indefinite leave to remain in the UK. If he is unable to find suitable employment, he plans to study for a Master's degree, which he hopes will give him the same labour market advantage of having studied for a year in the USA.

Savalan enjoyed being a university student. He met many new people but still mainly socialised with his refugee friends, some of whom he met in Dover and some in Brighton. He describes them as being really good friends whom he can count on, but often felt he should move away from them because they were not helping him with his academic studies. They would come home from work and want to just 'chill out', whereas he needed to study when he got home from work.

Being a full-time student was not without its sacrifices. He worked for a security company twenty hours a week but often found it hard to meet his financial commitments and felt he could do more. He described the difference between himself and some of his fellow students:

> For them it is a different story. They phone daddy or mummy and they give them money. In my turn my mummy or daddy phone me, and they ask me for money, so it's slightly different!

He described his responsibility for his family as 'quite a lot of pressure', but it is a responsibility that he has carried since he set up his own business, although he found it much easier in Iran. As the only son, it is his responsibility to make the decisions and support his parents financially. He talks of perhaps selling some of their land to relieve the financial pressure because he feared that his studies would suffer.

> I'll sort it out, I'm a fighter! I'm really happy that I'm helping my family, I don't want my parents to have a hard time because of money. Money is nothing, I will find money later and I can't find my parents later. You can't find a British person like that and I don't think they can understand because they don't understand my country. People there have to sort out their own problems, the government doesn't help.

The financial pressure Savalan was under increased when his two younger sisters started at university and he had to take financial responsibility for them too. He had become increasingly concerned that working as a security guard in night clubs could lead him into a violent confrontation, which in turn could bring him into contact with the police. Desperately concerned about his perceived vulnerable status, he started working twenty hours a week at a restaurant, and only two nights a week as a security guard. He also moved from his one-bedroom flat to smaller and cheaper accommodation.

During our interviews Savalan frequently talked of feeling homesick. His mother had suffered with poor mental health since he left and has had to be hospitalised several times. He describes the culture of sons getting married and bringing the new wife to live with or near their parents, supporting and caring for them in their old age. For his mother, Savalan's leaving was a terrible shock, from which she has never fully recovered.

> For her it was like her son died. Her son left and he won't be there again and I think it is very strong. You gave birth to lots of children to have a son, you got one and you lost him, yes?

He is particularly close to one of his sisters to whom he can talk and turn to for support. But his parents have been too distressed and too worried about him to offer any kind of support and he describes how on some telephone calls his mother just weeps. For Savalan, life in exile involves managing and reconciling different aspects of his identity: being an only son and brother, a worker and financial provider, a student and, increasingly, having a possible identity as a temporary sojourner here. His habitus is marked by both his Iranian culture and his refugee identity. He admits that sometimes trying to manage his feelings gets too much for him and he needs to withdraw and spend time on his own, away from everyone and everything. His story is a reminder that alongside establishing a new life as an immigrant, every refugee has a past life: they have left behind family, friends, culture and a community, and these are powerful bonds which continue to connect them with 'home'. This emigrant experience has profound affective and practical impact on their daily lives.

When I asked Savalan whether he felt a sense of belonging in the UK, he replied that it 'depends'.

> I didn't have any problems here because it's such a lovely place, cosmopolitan, people are really open-minded. I didn't have any problem that I'm from a different country, that I shouldn't be here.

He recounted an incident which had happened three weeks earlier in the early hours of the morning while he was waiting for his bus home. He was approached by a group of young white men, who asked him where he was from. When he refused to tell them they physically assaulted him and threw drink over him. It was only the arrival of the bus and the quick thinking of the driver, who opened the door just long enough for him to jump on, which saved him from a serious attack.

> When something like that happens I definitely, I definitely feel that you are not belonging to this country, this land, this nation.

He concluded by explaining that belonging depended on who he was with and 'whether they see differences of nationality, or whether I'm with shallow minded people'. Despite describing his experiencing what was a blatantly racist attack, Savalan is keen to try and explain and justify what had happened. He speculated that perhaps the three men had been beaten by a foreigner in the past, or that the attack might not have been because he was a foreigner but just because English people just like to pick fights late at night.

Savalan had to think carefully about whether or not he would ever go back to Iran. In the end he concluded that even if he were able to go back at some point in the future he wouldn't want to live there again. He could go back for two weeks or a month to see his family but that is all. He says he couldn't stand the ideas and the way people think and 'the way they talk to you, the way they treat you, the way they think of you and the way they socialise'. He was not optimistic about the Iranian uprising in June 2009 and described it as being more about a power struggle between members of the Government than any real change. He talked of how much he has changed in the last five years, 'a 180 degree change', which he puts down to education and lecturers encouraging students to 'go away and find things out and to question things'. He feels that he is 'a different person now', so could never imagine returning to Iran, although equally, he is not sure whether he wants to stay in the UK and would quite like to go to China or the USA. But this will depend on what happens when his visa expires.

8

Alan: the Iranian civil engineer's story

When I first interviewed Alan, he was a student on the WILAW course. His central concern and priority was to be able to work in the UK as a civil engineer. At first he was confident that he'd be able to work in his profession, but recognised he had a problem with the language. He felt he needed to focus on learning English and finding out what qualifications he needed to work as a civil engineer. He had only relatively recently been granted refugee status and the experience of his journey to the UK, and of being an asylum seeker, dominated our early interviews. His narrative foregrounds the horror of sudden flight and his fear at finding himself in an unfamiliar environment in which he could not imagine a future. From his passage from being a dispersed asylum seeker to becoming a student in higher education, Alan's narrative illuminates the anguish which can underlie and impact upon the process of transition and reorientation to life in exile. Dealing with the consequences of trauma have severely limited his opportunities for accruing and converting capital across different social sites.

Life in Iran

Alan was born in Mahabad in the mid 1970s. His father was a businessman who owned a small cake factory and shops and was involved in construction and property development. His mother devoted her life to running the home and raising five children; he describes her as being an artist and talented dressmaker, who could paint and also design and create clothes. Alan talks of his parents as literate but having had little formal education.

He grew up in Mahabad, a small city in north-west Iran close to the border with Iraq, which in the 1940s developed into the headquarters of the movement for Kurdish autonomy. Alan is proud of coming from the city which in 1945 became the capital of the autonomous Republic of Kurdistan. The republic was short lived however, lasting just one year before the Shah's regime arrested and executed the leaders. Alan explains that the Kurds' problem is not just a recent one with the Islamic Republic, but stretches back to the Shah's regime and even earlier. The Kurdish people '... have always been in conflict with the main government because they want their land back and they want their rights as well'.

Alan's childhood was dominated by wars. His earliest memory is of the civil war between the Iranian government and Kurdish opposition groups. Several Kurdish groups had been involved in armed struggle against the Government since 1979. In 1982 the Iranian Government launched a major attack and by the end of 1983 they had recaptured virtually all rebel held territory (Keddie, 2003). Government forces bombed Mahabad and he recalls the sandbags at the windows and how the family would hide in the cellar when the bombs fell. His family house had a large cellar and neighbours and people on the street had once run to his cellar for cover when the bombing started and had ended up staying for three or four nights. There was no electricity and people were packed so tightly together it was impossible to move. Although he was too young to fight in the Iran-Iraq war, Alan witnessed the war first hand as the city was attacked three times by Iraqi forces.

Compared to the political conflict and wars surrounding his childhood, Alan's school life passed uneventfully and he went to university to study civil engineering. His interest in it stemmed from visiting construction sites with his father as a boy. Although his father had no formal training or education he was, according to Alan, a good engineer who could draw up plans and do the calculations for buildings.

It was his father's dream that his children would be well educated and attend university. His father was so keen for him to attend school as soon as possible that he obtained Alan's documents one year early so that he could start school a year early. Alan proudly recounts that all his siblings are well educated: his brother is a civil engineer, one sister is an accountant, one has just graduated and his youngest sister is studying psychology at University. Alan combined university studies with working part-time as an engineering assistant at the local council – a job he got through family connections.

As soon as he completed university, Alan went to Tehran to do his military service. Twenty-one months of military service was compulsory for all Iranian men no matter what their ethnic background. Alan describes how Kurds in the military were treated differently from other Iranians. For example, after basic training they weren't allowed to choose which city they served their military service in, and were restricted in where they could work. After four months of basic training, Alan was sent to work in a civil engineering department in a city nine hours away from his home town. Despite the discrimination faced by Kurds, he regards his experience in the military as 'a good experience for life'. He was responsible for organising the work of 75 soldiers in the construction field and recounts how he gained experience not only of working on a variety of civil engineering projects but also of managing people.

Once he completed his military service, Alan returned to his home town and got a job as a civil engineer, working long hours on a large construction site. He describes how he had to be there before the workers and builders arrived and leave after them in the evening. It was a private company where most of the employees were Baha'is, a religious minority group which, like the Kurds, experienced economic and social discrimination. He enjoyed the job and gained broad experience of the construction industry, from surveying and setting up the site, to dealing with inspectors. He did this job for three years, until he had to flee to the UK.

Learning and living in the UK

Alan arrived in the UK in 2003. His journey had been on foot and in a box under a lorry.

> It was really dangerous; it was horrible. Even if I think about it now, my body is shaking. It was a really horrible experience in my life.

Both leaving and the journey were traumatic. He had never planned to leave Iran; it just happened, and it happened very suddenly:

> It was sudden, 100 per cent sudden ... there was no plan, no decision, nothing really ... If you make a plan and make a decision it is much easier for a person. For example, if you decide you want to go and live in Spain, you see it, you relax. Where in Spain? Looking on internet, search accommodation, if you can afford it, if you happy there or not. It all goes smoothly if you decide to go somewhere, if you plan to leave somewhere because you are mentally ready for the things that are going to happen to you. But when things happen suddenly you go from one part of the world psht straight to another part of the world. It's like a dream, you wake up 'Oh, another world'. It is very difficult, especially when you don't know the language, it is difficult to communicate, people can hardly understand you; it's a bit hard.

Reflecting back to the time before his flight from Iran, he found the idea that he might one day end up living in another country strange and almost amusing:

> I couldn't really imagine living in another country. No way, no never, really. When I was, okay when I was talking to someone in some other country I would feel sorry for them, I don't know why. Believe me, ha ha! Maybe, somehow I had a good life there, that's why I was okay, I was comfortable. I had my family next to me, I had my job, I had my fun. Everything, it was good, lots of adventures. Yeah.

Alan arrived in Dover and after a month was dispersed to Birmingham where he remained for a year and a half while his asylum claim was looked into by the Home Office. He didn't know anybody in Birmingham, but in line with National Asylum Support System (NASS) policy of trying to 'cluster' language and ethnic groups together, he was moved to several different hostels or houses, usually with Kurds from Iraq.

> The people around me, nobody thought about studying, just working. I tried to find my own way to learn English – talking, speaking. It's difficult when you are in a society and you cannot speak and can't say anything. You can't solve your problems. It's very difficult also when you ask interpreters, it takes a long time and may be impossible. I tried to go to college at that time by myself. The other problem is that the cultures are completely different, and the personality is different. I was in a home in Birmingham so the people around me were Kurdish from Iraq. Their personality and culture was not very interesting to me and I was annoyed by them. The

> difference between people: they came from another culture. Every time I was studying they ... I was from a culture of university and literate people at that time I was with people who didn't know anything about these things. They weren't educated. So I wanted to be with people who can understand each other. It was very difficult at that time to live with those people. They were drinking, shouting and things like that. It was very difficult to stay there but I had to stay there, I didn't have any choice. It was very difficult to study. As soon as I had my decision [Home Office decision to grant refugee status] I moved to get away to somewhere where I thought there would be people like me.

Alan came to the UK with what he described as 'kind of basic English'. As he said, he worked hard while in Birmingham to try and learn English from the television and the internet. He describes how he 'learnt a lot, but still couldn't communicate because there was no one to talk to'. Like Savalan, Alan was fortunate that asylum seekers could still attend Government funded ESOL courses.

> I went to [name] College. It was a full time course, I did an exam and they put me in the upper intermediate class. It was very difficult for me because the exam was just written. I am quite good at guessing words, probably because of that they put me in the upper intermediate. It was difficult for me, I was quite shy and I wouldn't communicate very well. Even if I didn't understand I wouldn't ask. I don't know – somehow I was new, new people, new students, I don't know. It was a busy class. I was afraid if I said anything it would be a mess! But step-by-step I got better and I was going to college five days a week. It was a very good college ... and the teachers were really good as well, very helpful. But unfortunately during this time, moving here, go there, go there I couldn't finish the course, but it was very useful.

Alan had no expectations of the UK and his memory of the first year as an asylum seeker is of a frightening and dark time:

> It was really scary for me at the beginning. Very scary and I don't know why but at the beginning I was thinking that I could never live here. It was a very difficult time ... when I started university here I felt I am living now somehow, but before that it wasn't really a life. It wasn't really a good life. Worrying, stress. I couldn't like open my mind to see around me because it was very difficult, and depressing. But okay when I started the University I joined your [WILAW] group and things, I gradually felt better and better.
>
> LM. What worried and stressed you when you first arrived here?

> A. When I go back to when I first arrived here, okay I don't know how to say how I feel. I didn't know what was going to happen. I didn't know what was going to happen really because already I, like we say, I washed my hands of my life in Iran. And when I arrived here I had the same feeling and that feeling was with me because I didn't know, somehow I was thinking okay I can never see my family again and that was always in my mind. I won't be able to see them again and that is it. It's a horrible feeling. When I think about it, it is a bit strange now [shuffles in chair]. I was thinking that I was going to die every day. I don't know why. Because it was a lot of pressure on me, a lot of stress. And okay every hour I was expecting that something would happen to me. It was like a shock to be honest, like a big shock. When I go back and think about those times I don't know. Some days it is hard and it is funny, both [laughs].
>
> LM. It sounds terrifying.
>
> A. It was really. It was and that's why I think this is still the side effects from that particular time that sometimes is still annoying me, do you know what I mean?

Alan's fragility and fear is palpable in his narrative; he'd turned his back on his past and yet cannot imagine a future. For an asylum seeker, only the most basic, subsistence level of support is available. The process of integration does not start until refugee status is confirmed (see chapter two). The transition from asylum seeker to refugee was difficult and Alan's story highlights the need for support during this period of transition from support by NASS to independent living or welfare benefits. As soon as refugee status was granted, he was given 28 days to leave the accommodation provided by NASS and find his own. He describes not knowing what to do and where to go, as he knew no one in Birmingham, apart from the people he was sharing a house with. He ended up staying on in the house beyond the 28 days, which he considered to have been 'illegal'. Unfortunately, most of the other people living there were refused asylum and had to leave the house and – officially – the country. These people then just 'disappeared', becoming part of the unknown number of undocumented 'illegal' migrants. Alan was left with no contacts in Birmingham and nowhere to stay.

While waiting for his claim for asylum to be processed he had looked into the possibility of working as a civil engineer. He discovered that his cultural capital could not be exchanged for employment reward and that he would have to study further to practise as an engineer.

> I didn't really want to do any other job. I've seen other people who had qualifications from their country and they do other jobs like making a business or working in a pizza shop or factory rather than their own specialism, and I didn't want to be like that. I want to work as an engineer. The only thing I could do was think about going to university and getting an engineering qualification and getting a job.

Alan had already looked at higher education courses and decided that as soon as he received his status he would study at university. He was attracted to Brighton because it had two universities, and through his family in Iran he discovered that there was a family friend living in Brighton. He moved to the south coast but, because he could not pay the deposit and rent in advance for private accommodation, he spent seven months staying firstly at this friend's house and then living in his car. It was at this point that he joined the WILAW course. He had already identified a Masters programme and had made a direct approach to the course leader to study for a Masters degree in civil engineering. Through his direct approach, and probably his enthusiasm and determination, he was offered a place on the Masters, providing he improved his English.

He continued to study English at a local college and took an advanced course which gave him a certificate equivalent to the IELTS he needed for entry to the MSc. Alan was eventually housed by the Local Authority just before he started his degree. He was aware of the cultural capital which having a UK university qualification provided and cited gaining a qualification as his main motivation for going to university in the UK.

> I thought the course would be very, very difficult for me because of the language. I thought I might need a lot of time translating and learning at the same time but it wasn't like that really. The first semester I was worried that I might not be able to pass the modules, but I studied and I really didn't need to translate much. So the first semester I had two modules and I passed them so I got a big confidence inside myself.

I asked him whether the experience of being a student had changed him. His response was immediate and confident:

> Yes! I'm really ready to do another course [laughs]. Really I'm enjoying it. I wasn't so confident when I started university, at the first point, but now I can apply for any course that I like and I can do it. Yeah, yeah. It's a big change for me. ... I really enjoyed the feeling of being a student again. You

> know? [laughs] After a long time and I'd still like to be a student and I'm worried about when I finish my degree and lose the university. I'd like to be there all the time. It's a nice feeling. It's a nice environment.

When asked what made it so special, he identified the sense of common purpose and being part of something:

> When you are all in a place that you [pause] everyone is coming for a reason to get the knowledge, to get the qualifications, to know more about things ... Somehow being a student makes you ... er, it makes you feel younger [laughs].

For Alan, being a student at university represented more than a means to a qualification. It gave him an alternative positive identity, that of being a full time student, and was significant on a personal and emotional level. It gave him a sense of personal agency and meaning at a time when forced migration had led to the disintegration of any biographical certainties he may have felt as a young person in Iran. Giddens (1991) describes how late modernity constantly precipitates crises of self, but at the same time creates opportunities for individuals to construct their own meanings and biographies – what he refers to as the 'reflexive project of the self'. Similarly, West (1996), in his biographical study of adults in higher education, describes how education can be an emotional and intellectual resource, helping participants move beyond the fragments of their past lives.

> Higher Education is potentially a space in which to manage and transcend feelings of marginalisation, meaninglessness and inauthenticity in interaction with others; in which it is possible ... to compose a new life, a different story and a more cohesive self. (1996:10)

Although being a student gave Alan a sense of worth and source of respect, he was very different from his fellow students. Only in his late twenties he was nonetheless older than most, and most of the others were from European countries or the far East. Unlike them, he was having to support himself, delivering fast food and working as an interpreter. While the formal, taught aspect of being a university student had a levelling effect: 'everyone is the same so it's fine', the broader experience of being a student was marked by differences in habitus and differentials in financial resources and in motivation. He felt some of his fellow students had 'come here just for the fun and not for studying';

they had parties and went out most nights. It was a lifestyle that he couldn't afford to be part of:

> When I was in that situation sometimes I would say that I can't drink, or I can't go out, I feel sick or I'm doing things. I know that they spend a lot of money and I can't afford it.

Alan successfully completed his MSC in two years. He had even hoped to do so in one year, but health issues intervened and he had 'had some other problems to sort out'. He joined the Graduate Institute of Civil Engineering, wanting 'to be a proper civil engineer in the practical world'. On paper he had re-established his identity as a civil engineer, but on an affective and practical level, that identity remained fragile and insecure.

Alan has spent the two years since completing his degree applying for 'hundreds' of jobs as a civil engineer, and not being shortlisted or invited for interview for any. We met informally several times during this period to look at his CV and covering letter, and to discuss possible strategies for gaining employment. He was concerned that prejudice towards his Iranian nationality and ethnic identity could be a factor and this was the prime motivation for applying for and gaining British citizenship. Despite formally gaining the new national identity to put on his CV, he was keenly aware that he could not hide or disguise the fact that he had spent the first twenty-seven years of his life in Iran.

Bourdieu describes how codes of distinction are used to perpetuate and reinforce systematic patterns of domination and subordination. In Alan's case we see how race and ethnicity work as markers of habitus and serve to generate distinction, functioning as negative symbolic capital (Bourdieu, 1998:104). Despite his UK academic credentials and formal membership of a professional group, his habitus marks him off as different and other, and the distance between professional employment and his racialised identity cannot be bridged. He recognises these classifying practices and how in the field of professional employment they position him in an inferior and unequal position. The symbolic power of 'Whiteness' and of the cultural practices associated with having a habitus indigenous to the field in question are recognised as legitimate and natural. Through such symbolic violence Alan's subordination is perpetuated and institutionalised.

During his five years in the UK Alan has struggled with periods of depression and nightmares which he feels are connected to his past. This trauma has disrupted his ability to accrue and convert capital across different sites, and at times he feels he has been here for five years and 'achieved nothing'. He misses his family, particularly his youngest sister. His parents have visited him in the UK once, but he has missed the weddings of three of his siblings and has nephews and nieces in Iran whom he's never seen. In our penultimate interview he said his goal was to try and establish better contact with his family and that he hoped this would help him to 'get his energy back'. He had applied for a British passport, which would make it easier to travel than using his Home Office documents, and his plan was to travel and meet his family in a third country.

Earlier on in our interviews Alan had found it hard to imagine going back to Iran. It was difficult for him to remember what his life there had been like and he didn't trust the image of the life he had had. He was afraid that if he went back he would have to 'start from the beginning again'. I last met Alan in summer 2009. He felt excited and optimistic about the uprising in Iran and hoped there would be changes in the country which might enable him to return. The interview was tinged with nostalgia, possibly influenced by his feelings of powerlessness, when he told me he would 'love to go back'. Although he worked longer hours in Iran, he felt it was an easier place to live in and he didn't feel so alone. But he would only go back if it is safe.

At the moment, Alan feels that additional security is applied to refugees who have left and this makes him feel more vulnerable. Becoming a British citizen makes him feel 'freer', as he can travel abroad more easily and he is hopeful that it might bring him advantages in the labour market. He expressed huge disappointment that, despite his MSc, he cannot secure work as a civil engineer. He is thinking about studying again and was concerned to identify a course most likely to lead to a job. His priorities are changing, as his desperation to find any professional employment grows:

> Maybe petrochemical engineering, computer engineering, mechanical engineering? Anything to get a job, any job ...

At the moment Alan doesn't feel settled in the UK because he doesn't have a job or 'a pattern to his life'. He has a girlfriend whom he has been seeing for just over a year. He describes their relationship as being 'very serious', but he couldn't contemplate marriage until he has a job.

In Alan's story we see how the processes of transition and self-reconstruction are far from linear or straightforward. Rather, it is characterised by flux and uncertainty, and an interweaving of feelings of impotence and agency, marginality and belonging. His position and experience as a student gave him the opportunity to exercise personal agency and to compose a positive identity and subjectivity. During this period his narrative is optimistic and he can begin to imagine a future and a life in the UK working as a civil engineer. Sadly, the UK qualification by which he had set so much store has not opened doors to professional employment, as he hasn't the power to capitalise on it. Either side of being a university student, his narrative is characterised by a sense of powerlessness, and in our last interview, despite having acquired British citizenship and a British passport, he was less certain than before of his future in the UK. His later interviews reflected nostalgia for Iran and a desire to be able to return: past memories of Iran were being re-conceptualised in the light of an uncertain and structureless present.

9

The role of asylum policy and public discourses in learning and identity processes

The narratives in the last five chapters describe and document the experiences of five people as they learned to live in the UK as asylum seekers and refugees. This chapter seeks to link the individual narratives to the broader social structures and practices, and to bring to the surface the social and political processes at work in the construction and re-construction of refugee identities and subjectivities. As C. Wright Mills (1959) asserts, 'personal troubles' must be understood as 'public issues' if we are to make a difference in the quality of human life in our times.

We saw how the five subjects recognised 'asylum seeker' and 'refugee' as categories which fundamentally defined how other people perceived them and which acutely influenced how they were responded to and treated. The work of Bourdieu (1977; 1998) suggests that policy and social discourses can be thought of as schemes of perception and classification which symbolically construct certain groups as inferior, and ensure that relations of subordination and domination are reproduced. In the case of refugees, these systems ensure that they are constructed as lacking in qualities necessary to generate valuations of self respect, dignity or moral worth. Faced with such symbolic disparagement, refugees draw on alternative discourses and education strategies as a means of articulating positive and meaningful subjectivities and identities for themselves.

Imposed identities: moving through the asylum system

Given the social and political discourses around asylum issues, it is not surprising that most of the participants in this research wished to conceal their identity – as asylum seeker and refugee – and keep it secret. Only Maryam found the identity of refugee unproblematic; she appeared happy to 'own' this identity. For her the onset of migration had been a gradual process which took place in the context of years of persecution and human rights abuses in Iraq. Once in the UK, being granted refugee status was swift and uncomplicated. Unlike other participants, she had not been left in the limbo of being an asylum seeker. Although she misses her extended kinship group, Maryam is part of a family unit in the UK and has close family bonds. These bonds not only represent cultural resources which provide mutual support and purpose, but they are also a means of constructing herself as having value and worth: she is a good mother and wife, doing her best firstly to reunite, and then to support, her family. Her fear for the future of her children in Iraq was the final trigger in her decision to leave, and although she has never mentioned the greater opportunities that are available to her children in the UK, and the greater capital that accompanies a UK education, this is also likely to influence how she feels about the status of being a refugee.

In contrast, Patricia arrived in the UK on her own and had to negotiate a series of imposed identities which significantly impacted on her subjectivity. As we see below her arrival narrative describes the fluidity of the immigration statuses and labels that she moves through in her first year here, and how she negotiated the identities imposed upon her. Coming from Zimbabwe, she was initially granted a visitor's visa as she couldn't bring herself to declare that she was seeking asylum.

> I just couldn't do it at the airport. I thought 'Oh my goodness, no I can't do this!' So the person at the counter actually asked 'You're from Zimbabwe, things there are not very good'. I said 'Yeah things are not very good'. 'Are you visiting somebody?' I don't know why, but I just said 'yes'. I remember I was given one month. I came out and I didn't even have anywhere to go.

Patricia had one telephone number, that of someone her sister had met when she was in the UK eleven years before. Through this contact she ended up sharing a room with a Zimbabwean woman. But even then it took her four months to summon the courage to apply for asylum. Her reluctance was compounded by the horror stories told by her flat mate who advised her against it:

> She was just like 'But what if you are denied? And what if you are detained? And maybe you won't be able to call your family from one of those centres. And people don't know when people have been detained and people are held in circumstances which are not very humane'. And I thought that 'Oh my goodness I'm going to go to jail now'. She was describing it like she had been there and she had some, someone who had been. So it took me some time.

In the period before she applied for asylum, Patricia found paid employment with care agencies and care homes. This area of work is the largest single occupational category for Zimbabweans in the UK (Bloch, 2005 cited in McGregor, 2007). Privatisation and contracting out have created unstable and insecure employment conditions and low wages, which have increased the use of migrants to do the work in this industry. 'Informal recruitment practices' have flourished, enabling newly arrived migrants to work, but also allowing for their exploitation (McGregor, 2007).

Patricia was aware that with an expired visitor's visa it was illegal to work but felt she had no choice. She had arrived in the UK with £375 and had to pay her rent, bills and buy food. Each time she applied for a job she would tell the employer that she had sent her passport to the UK Home Office and was waiting for it to be returned. Every week her employer would ask for her passport and every week Patricia would say that it was with the Home Office. After a few months she would leave that agency and start the process again with a new employer.

> Yes it was illegal, it was illegal. That's what I'm saying, I'm not sure whether they didn't know that this was illegal because obviously they didn't even see my passport, but they still gave me a job.

Patricia finally did apply for asylum and felt relieved because it made her feel slightly 'more legal'. However, as an asylum seeker she was still legally excluded from the labour market and had to continue her precarious and illegal employment.

> I think I was more anxious before I had filed for asylum, I was more anxious because you are an illegal somebody. It is worse than being an asylum

> seeker who was waiting a decision, you are, you know it is illegal and the employer possibly knows it is illegal, and the pay rates were very low as well. Very low as well. ... And people back home, I mean six or seven months down the line and you're still not sending any money. It doesn't go down well, you know? ... Every day you thank God after every shift because you know because you've worked you're going to be paid for it. After every shift you thank God because that's something at the end of the month. I didn't even have a bank account. I was using this lady, who I used to live with, I was using her bank account. She gave me her card, so I was using her card at the ATM ... Not even anybody back home can ever imagine me or anyone doing that. ... There's no way you can actually make anyone understand what you went through. There's no way. The lies that you tell, the anxiety, oh goodness, it was really ... it's funny looking back now and you think 'My goodness, how did I do all that, how did I get away with that?' It is a very long time to wait. You don't want to go back there to being an illegal and having your boss there asking for your passport every other week or every other day. Oh my goodness, how long can it take?

As she moved through the sequence of imposed identities of undocumented migrant, asylum seeker and eventually refugee, Patricia's choices and activities were differentially constrained and her identities transformed. She subverted these identities, as firstly a 'visitor', then an undocumented migrant and then an asylum seeker, by working illegally.

Although none of the participants drew attention in their narrative to having taken paid employment while waiting for their asylum claim to be processed, four of the five had done so. Farideh describes how the social services were 'very nice', how they found them somewhere safe and quiet to stay, arranged medical treatment for her and gave them vouchers for food. But they forgot about clothes and the other personal items she might need. Farideh had arrived with just the clothes she was wearing and had to stay in bed while these were washed and dried. She very apologetically admitted that she had taken a job, as a cleaner in a hotel, despite knowing that it was illegal. Effectively she, like a great many migrants, had become a circumstantial law breaker – identities and behaviour which were far from anything she could have imagined before she came to the UK. It also reinforces the morally problematic associations with refugee identity, making it virtually impossible to generate valuations of being a moral subject.

For all of them the identity of asylum seeker was associated with vulnerability, shame and waiting, so it was something to be kept firmly hidden from anyone else. Patricia sums up the feelings expressed by other participants:

> It's funny, British people are not very friendly to asylum seekers so it's not something that you just lay on the table and say 'Oh I'm an asylum seeker, I've got problems at home'. You don't. Like I said I never got any [state] benefit I don't even know why. But people have the impression that asylum seekers get all these benefits and they don't go to work and they get all this free housing ... it is embarrassing, I still feel that. I don't tell anybody.

Her depiction of the negative and stereotyped images surrounding the asylum seeker identity echoes Zetter's point that the asylum seeker label transforms an identity into a politicised image; it is not a neutral way of describing the world, but has the covert intention to '... convey an image of marginality, dishonesty, a threat, unwelcomed ...' (2007: 184). Despite these symbolic representations, these participants resist the attempt to define and secure identities in various ways, as they struggle to be recognised as having moral worth. Patricia, for example, constructs herself in opposition to this dominant and problematic script; her presentation of self is as being strong and resilient, and her narrative emphasises agency, determination and extraordinary hard work, as she manages to provide for herself and her family in the UK and at home. Through claiming an identity as hard working, caring and respectable, she is able to legitimate her distinction from symbolic representations and to claim moral authority.

Both Savalan and Alan had experienced dispersal. For Savalan it had been a relief to leave Dover and the hostilities he experienced there. He was moved with some of the Iranians he'd made friends with in the hostel, so he had support in finding his way in a new city. Almost five years later he was still friends with some of those people so they were clearly significant relationships for him. This was in total contrast to Alan's experience of dispersal. He had been housed with other Kurds but they were very different from him: 'they weren't educated' and had different aspirations so 'it was very difficult to study [while living with them]'. For Alan being an asylum seeker was a lonely and frightening time. He wasn't able to build any close or supportive relationships with the other Kurds around him and his English was not good enough for him to establish other relationships easily. He felt he had 'washed [his] hands of [his] life in Iran', but the ascribed identity of asylum seeker and exclusion from capital trading sites did not enable him to start building a new life or imagining a new identity for himself in the UK. Fortunately, asylum seekers could still access Government funded ESOL classes then, so he was able to attend classes and accrue capital, although his learning was disrupted by having to move hostels. It was a deeply stressful time for Alan and compounded the trauma surrounding his sudden flight and journey to the UK. Like many refugees, Alan has struggled with mental health issues directly related to becoming a refugee and these have continued to impact on his efforts to integrate.

From asylum seeker to refugee: gaining status?

For those who had spent longest seeking asylum, it was an enormous relief when their refugee status was confirmed and they could finally start making plans for their future. Alan moved to a different city, attracted by the two universities and the hope of being with people he might have more in common with. For Patricia it meant an end to her identity as 'illegal worker'; she finally had legal access to the labour market and better rates of pay. However, despite the changed label and legal entitlements which becoming a refugee conferred, her new identity, like that of asylum seeker, was still associated with embarrassment and subject to dissimilation. Becoming a refugee was not a more morally acceptable identity; the affective dimension did not change, only the legal identity.

We saw that Savalan blamed the British media and Government for only ever highlighting the problems associated with refugees and the rare incidences of law breaking or alleged terrorist activities, rather than the positive contribution made by the vast majority. He was concerned that people would look down on him or pity him if they knew he was a refugee, and only ever described himself as a 'student'. Even after he had been at university for two years he did not confide in any of his fellow students that he was a refugee. Similarly Alan describes being cautious about making new friends. He describes how he had learned to be careful about how he chose his friends and that 'you cannot trust a person at the first point'. Eventually he told some of his student friends that he was a refugee, but only once they had got to know what sort of person he was.

Farideh describes her humiliation when she went to register for an advanced English language course and the secretary of the English for Foreign Languages (EFL) department announced loudly in front of all the others in the queue behind her:

> We haven't got anywhere for refugees and asylum seekers. You have to wait, come back in two weeks, but I don't promise anything.

Farideh explains that the other students in the queue would be paying high fees for the course. She was being told to come back once enrolments had finished to see if there was a place left which she could take up at a reduced cost. She left the college and promised herself never to go back to the EFL department. She clearly felt the problem lay in the asylum seeker/refugee label rather than merely being foreign or different. Like Savalan, she blamed the media for their pejorative portrayal of asylum seekers.

Patricia too was concerned about how she would be perceived if she identified herself as a refugee. Like Farideh, she attributed blame to the popular discourses which associate refugees with being dependent on state benefits and not contributing to the community:

> On official forms, when they ask for immigration status, that's the only place you tick the 'refugee', because obviously they need to know that you can work. Everywhere else, no, no. I never tell anyone unless I have to do because otherwise people start to look at you differently. They start looking at you as if you are someone who is benefiting from the state and not giving anything, you know? So you wouldn't want people to look at you like that cos you're not benefiting anything as such, you are also contributing to whatever you are doing. It's not like you're getting weekly or monthly benefits or living in a house for free.

Symbolic struggles and the generation of moral worth

These narratives indicate that participants were painfully aware that to be an asylum seeker or a refugee was morally problematic and a source of stigma. They were concerned about refugee identity in terms of what it said about their worth. Much of their struggle was to do with wanting to be seen as respectable and creating distance from representations of themselves as pathological. The negative social definitions and associations imposed by powerful discourses contrast sharply with the self definitions and identities constructed by refugees themselves.

Embedded within these discourses and social definitions are the discriminatory structures and practices which establish and maintain the subordinate positioning of refugees. Bourdieu's concept of symbolic violence is based on such 'socially inculcated beliefs' or 'collective expectations' (1998:103). Policy and public discourses are inscribed with schemes of perception and classification which establish and sustain the inferiority of refugees. These serve to legitimate and reproduce the social order and the relations of subordination and domination embedded in it. In the case of asylum seekers and refugees these mechanisms include their exclusion from the labour market and the education system, and the discursive practices of stereotyping refugees as 'benefit scroungers', criminals and potential terrorists. Such social markers form part of the symbolic order and are used to marginalise and justify the differential treatment of minorities, who then become the 'other'.

This otherness has been fuelled and reinforced by the UK media which has paid a great deal of attention to refugee issues, both before and after 9/11. Much of the media attention has generated negativity and panic about refugees and, as Kundnani (2001) argues, has created a climate where racism against refugees can pass unrecognised as racism and therefore remain unchallenged. Refugees are stigmatised and disadvantaged by the symbolic order; by vilifying refugees the media contributes to devaluing and delegitimating their capital, making it harder to convert into symbolic capital and limiting capacity to accrue other capitals. Both policy and the media serve as institutional mechanisms which work to establish and maintain inequality, producing symbolic violence against refugees.

Despite this policy context, and against these wider social, political and public discourses and concerns, the refugees featured in this book demonstrate remarkable resilience in the way they have attempted to resist the limited and limiting subject positions, to forge their own self-definition and write their own identity scripts. The socially available ontological narratives or scripts were, in various ways, rejected by the participants, who tended to highlight values and beliefs in direct opposition to these discourses. In the absence of discourses which might enable them to articulate being a refugee as a positive identity, the values they weave through these narratives are of agency, education, responsibility, hard work, the wish to contribute and give back, as they strive to reposition themselves.

These refugees were all hugely concerned to be seen as respectable. The privileged habitus and class position in their country of origin had ensured that they were used to being accorded respect and respectability. The loss of this habituated respect was keenly felt. In Patricia's narrative we see how she rejects the stereotype that refugees are in the UK so they can claim benefits. She makes clear that she has never claimed benefits and her story emphasises the long hours she worked to support her family, both during her journey through the asylum system and later as a full time student.

Savalan is anxious to define himself in contrast to asylum seekers and refugees who come to the UK and don't learn English. He uses his proactive and committed approach to learning English to set boundaries between himself and other refugees, and to establish his identity as a good citizen, worthy of the right to remain in the UK. We also see this boundary work in his strategic decision to move to a different college, where he would be mixing with non-refugees. This was presented as an opportunity to learn more and to socialise with non-refugees, but also implies a distancing from his refugee friends who did not aspire to higher education and the level of integration he wanted to achieve. The issue re-emerged in an interview several years later when he was coming to the end of his first year as a university student, when he expressed the wish to spend more time with 'good students' rather than his refugee friends who didn't necessarily understand his need to study when he came home from work, rather than 'chill out' with them.

Alan was similarly keen to distance himself from the 'uneducated' asylum seekers with whom he had been dispersed to Birmingham and appeared less committed to studying than he was. He took the bold step of moving to a city he'd never been to, despite the homelessness that this entailed, in the hope of being able to find a community with whom he could identify.

This chapter has highlighted the conflict between the externally imposed identities of the symbolic order and the identities harboured and nurtured by the participants as they struggled to generate positive valuations for themselves and in relation to others. Despite the social positioning of asylum seekers being fixed and limiting, the participating refugees were all able to exercise agency in different ways. While dominant ideologies and symbolic systems have a damaging and constraining influence on refugees' subjectivities, they represent a counterpoint against which to construct and define themselves. By creating alternative self-definitions with positive valuations, the imposition of negative representations is resisted. The participants themselves recognised the legitimacy of classifying and positioning refugees as uneducated and lacking in aspiration to integrate or contribute to society. Through this misrecognition, the relations of dominance are internalised and perpetuated and the system's '... naturalisation of its own arbitrariness' (Bourdieu, 1977:164) is secured. The narratives indicate what Sayer (2005) calls complex 'moral boundary work' as participants seek to establish themselves as different from these 'undeserving' or 'unacceptable' refugees.

The stories also indicate how the struggle over identities and learning what it means to be an asylum seeker or refugee are part of a hidden curriculum. Participants learned how to enter the labour market without appropriate documentation and before they had a legal entitlement to work. We saw how negative stereotypes are assimilated and learned informally from the media, from encounters with others and their expectations and assumptions. Asylum seekers also learn through policy which constructs them as bogus and undeserving, until their claim for asylum is proven and accepted. The next chapter explores the informal learning processes at work, and how refugees engage with formal learning in strategies to re-establish professional identities and gain greater control over their lives.

10

Learning to live: informal and formal experiences of learning

The individual narratives presented in this book indicate the enormous amount of learning which accompanies the transition to living in the UK. Not all this learning is necessarily positive and most of it occurs outside formal education structures. The first part of this chapter explores the informal or incidental learning processes involved in transition to the UK. I suggest that there exists a subterranean or hidden curriculum of beliefs, expectations, norms, tacit assumptions and behaviours to be apprehended and learned as part of the transition process. This hidden curriculum is largely accessed through informal and non-formal learning, which is recognised as often being far more significant than formal, planned learning. When it comes to learning, the major frame of reference for adults is what they have experienced and practised in social groups, from watching others, from television, from work and so on.

Some of the strongest learning experiences in the five narratives occurred across a range of social sites and, in the case of Maryam and Patricia, through having to re-think and re-negotiate the gendered role of motherhood in a new space. Learning as described in chapter three is conceptualised as an inevitable part of life and as intimately linked to processes of becoming and identity formation. The second part of this chapter looks at the role of formal, planned learning in the transition process and how refugees have attempted to use higher education as a strategy to re-brand themselves and accrue exchangeable education capital.

Learning and transformation: the hidden curriculum

Mezirow's work on transformative learning (see chapter three) helps us to understand some of the learning processes in non-formal learning situations, particularly in situations of disjuncture in an individual's life (Mezirow, 1990; 2000). A major theme in the refugees' stories was the different cultural, social and political values and assumptions which they encountered in the UK. The theme of adapting to new cultural beliefs and expectations was particularly pronounced where the person was from a very different culture. To use Mezirow's framework, the historically and culturally constructed meaning schemes which participants brought with them did not sit comfortably in UK society and culture. This dissonance or 'disequilibrium' was sufficient to make them critically reflect on their tacit assumptions and beliefs and explore and alter their perspectives. This idea of disequilibrium echoes Bourdieu's notion of habitus becoming 'divided against itself' or Alheit and Dausien's metaphor of 'stumbling' or arriving at a 'crossroads' in our 'biographically acquired landscape' (Alheit and Dausien, 2002). For all these writers, such moments of discontinuity and disorientation suggest learning and transformation. I explore this notion of learning and transformation in relation to how individuals adapt to the cultural expectations of everyday life. However, this represents only part of the picture. There appear to be profound and contradictory learning processes concerned with identity and subject construction which are not captured by the notion of transformative learning.

Maryam describes the country she came from as being a 'closed culture' where the political, cultural and religious context was tightly circumscribed by the Government. There was little geographical movement of people within the country and they knew so little about what was going on outside it that she was even unaware that her brother had successfully applied for refugee status. Maryam describes how the political and religious ideas put forward by the Iraqi Government 'grow in your mind' and how difficult it is to comprehend and adapt to the ideas and culture of a more open and permissive society.

Similarly Savalan describes Iran as 'a prison and all the people are prisoners'. His narrative vividly portrays the shock and numbness, the 'disorientating dilemma' he experienced on arriving in the UK and being confronted with challenges to his assumptions and expectations.

He singles out seeing openly gay and lesbian couples for the first time and seeing people sitting at home alone watching television in the evenings, as being particularly unexpected and disconcerting. These narratives both emphasise the enormous amount of informal and incidental learning which living in a new and different culture demands.

Some refugees underwent this type of learning through the planned construction of spaces for informal learning. For example, Farideh participated in a 'Time Together' project funded by the UK Refugee Council which matches refugees in one-to-one mentoring relationships with local volunteers. It gave her an opportunity to talk about and explore aspects of British culture which she'd always been curious about. She described, for example, how she'd always wanted to go into a pub and had always 'looked inside from the outside, and I wanted to know what's happening inside'. Her mentor chose a very old pub with a real fire, and on the second attempt Farideh plucked up the courage to go inside. Together they went to the library and museums and on a boat trip; none of which she'd done in the preceding five years in the UK.

This illustrates the importance of informal and unstructured spaces which allow for recognition of the affective and social dimensions of adapting to a new culture. Similarly, the evaluation of the WILAW course (Morrice, 2009) highlighted the unanticipated outcomes which resulted from providing a forum for the exploration of different cultural, social and political values. Class discussions were identified as important opportunities to discuss and debate aspects of UK society and culture. The role of mentors was identified as not only providing specialist advice and guidance on particular career paths, but also providing insights into the culture and expectations of different fields of work. This underlines what adult educators know already, that is, the importance of social spaces for informal or spontaneous discussion and activities which arise in response to the quotidian life experiences of adults. Opportunities to discuss and explore different world views and cultural expectations with other students from diverse backgrounds supports the sense making necessary for learning to live in a different culture.

King (1999) found similar transformations in learners' understanding of culture and self in her study with ethnically and culturally mixed groups of English as Second Language students in the US. Drawing on the work of Mezirow, King describes how, alongside the language learning, participants reported significant cultural and personal transformation. This included greater cultural awareness, and in particular how preconceived ideas and beliefs about cultures were transformed. Her participants also reported how they gained greater self-esteem and sense of empowerment as they learnt to cope with learning a new language and culture. She suggests that such transformations are linked to particular activities which encourage critical thinking and discussion in a supportive environment.

Magro (2007) also draws on the work of Mezirow, to explore the experiences of adult learners from war affected countries now living in Canada. She argues that learning opportunities for refugees need to go beyond the functional skills of language learning and recognise the personal, social and cultural transformations which accompany adaptation to a new country.

The shock of a new culture was less intense for Maryam, as she had previously travelled in Europe and the US. She describes the differences between being a tourist, where you 'watch' and 'see' a different life, and actually living in new culture, which she saw as a more active process where you have to 'be melted with their culture', 'know everything about their culture, about their system, about everything in the life' (chapter four). She was determined to fit into UK society and her narrative suggests that she actively engages in boundary work to identify herself with the community she has entered. She purposefully transforms her frame of reference: adopting new roles and ways of acting in her relationship with her children and her husband, and in her professional practice as a teacher, and also to blend into wider UK society. In her narrative there is no sense of loss.

Savalan and Alan, however, both adopted an eclectic approach to UK culture – selecting aspects they liked and rejecting others. A strong theme in Savalan's narrative was his self-directed learning and his single mindedness in wanting to learn all he could about British culture and English language, from the moment he arrived in Dover. He was curious, for instance, to learn how Christmas was celebrated in the UK, and determined to learn English through watching television and making lists of new vocabulary. He approached the matter of learning strategically. He befriended the manager of the hotel in Dover and learned from her about British culture and where, for example he could buy the hard lumps of sugar he needed to make Iranian tea. Once settled with refugee status, he took the strategic decision to move to an English language course where he wouldn't be with other refugees. His suggestion that you can 'learn with them more' clearly recognises the importance of building diverse social networks and the informal learning that occurs within them (Field, 2005; Morrice, 2007).

Learning and (un)becoming

Implicit in all of these writings about learning and transformation is the suggestion that learning is generally positive and of benefit, and that it either builds on previous learning or offers a new and more suitable frame of reference. The transformations which accompany learning are assumed to enable the individual to understand and function more effectively and to adapt better to the new context. Some learning described in these narratives can be understood in this way – but much of it cannot. In particular this narrow view of learning doesn't capture or elucidate the ongoing process of identity formation which accompanies movement across social sites. There is a complexity and depth to the learning of refugees which is not always a linear process of building on previous learning, neither is it necessarily a positive or beneficial process. Rather, it is a contradictory and largely deconstructive process. Much learning is concerned with recognising that their previous learning counts for very little, and involves having to unlearn and let go of much of who, and what they were; it is concerned with subjectivity and with identity (de)construction.

Current understandings of learning are moving beyond theories of transmission and cognitive reconstruction (see chapter three). In line with this shift in focus Biesta (2006) argues that rather than seeing learning as the acquisition of something 'external', whether that is '... an attempt to acquire, to master, to internalise, we might see learning as an attempt to reorganise and reintegrate as a result of disintegration ...' (2006:27). Conceptualising learning as a response rather than as an acquisition, acknowledges that learning can have a disturbing impact and can entail a 'violation of the sovereignty of the student' (2006:29).

Similarly, Hodkinson *et al* (2007) draw on a Deweyan notion of embodied construction to argue for a view of learning as a process of 'becoming' or 'being'. They conceptualise learning as an ongoing construction of the self through participation. Avoiding the implicit assumption that learning is an entirely positive or constructive process, they suggest that learning is also about 'unbecoming' or ceasing to be something.

The refugee narratives presented here suggest that much learning is about 'unbecoming'; it is about learning what they are not, learning what is not legitimate and exchangeable, and about learning that, as refugees, they have little or no moral worth or value. They learn that from the stigmatised social position of refugee there are no socially available scripts or narratives upon which they can draw to construct and present themselves as worthy or moral beings. Instead they are engaged in a constant process of learning how to resist negative evaluations and generate distance from representations of themselves as pathological. Drawing on alternative discourses of caring, hard work, education and the good citizen, they learn how to feel and to present themselves as having value and moral worth in relation to others. Their narratives illuminate how, from the disintegration and deconstruction of self which accompanies migration, the participants learn to 'become', which in its broadest sense means they learn how to rethink themselves and live with integrity and dignity in a new social space. For all the refugees in this research, higher education in the UK was perceived as a means of constructing themselves as morally desirable and of beginning to re-build their professional identities.

Higher education as a strategy for accruing capital and worth

Once refugee status is confirmed, refugees can participate in educational opportunities on the same basis as their British counterparts. For the purposes of higher education they are treated as 'home students'; they pay home student fees and can apply for student loans. They are not tracked in higher education so we have little research information on their experiences within university. We do know that there are significant barriers to refugees getting their previous qualifications recognised and gaining access to university (Aldridge and Waddington, 2001; Waddington, 2005; Houghton and Morrice, 2008). It is probably one of the most significant examples of the cultural capital which refugees bring with them not being valued or recognised. We know that the journey into HE can be long and often complicated (Morrice, 2009). We also know that refugees, as we saw with Farideh (chapter six) often struggle with the unfamiliar expectations and practices of higher education, and can find the experience isolating and distressing (Houghton and Morrice, 2008; Stevenson, 2008).

The experience of higher education was different for each participant and this reflected the extent to which their capital was recognised and the adherence between habitus and the field of higher education. Patricia felt confident about her ability to cope with the academic demands of training to be a mental health nurse, but was somewhat concerned about the practical aspects, as she had no experience of working in mental health. In contrast to her experience of teacher training in Zimbabwe, where both her parents were teachers and where books and educational literature were readily available, she didn't know anyone who had studied mental health nursing.

She enjoyed the taught part of the course, particularly, as a teacher for eleven years, the 'enrichment of being on the receiving end'. The one aspect she did find difficult was the isolation of studying alone. She contrasts this with her experience of boarding school and residential teacher training college in Zimbabwe, where she took part in group discussions and shared literature and ideas with her fellow students. However, as her comments below indicate, she understood the personal tutor role and the importance of asking for help if needed, an understanding which is not present in Farideh's story.

> Really, just taking your books from the library and going to sit home with your essay and maybe just do it wrongly or anything like that you know. ... So it was really, really like, kind of a shock: you get an essay topic, you just go home and do it on your own. It was like, can I do this? But anyway I did, but yeah, that was really difficult. Of course you have your personal tutor who can support you if you need them, but you don't always want to use your personal tutor. They are available, they want you to use them because at the end of the day you might fail that essay and have to re-write so it is better to see your personal tutor than to have to re-write a new thing.

Patricia was pleasantly surprised to find there were a number of mature students on the course. They tried to establish a discussion group, but it never got up and running. The practical aspect of the course and the work placements were not as daunting as Patricia had imagined. She felt that her experience of care work had prepared her for joining a team as a novice and outsider and gradually becoming more confident. As a student mental health nurse on placement, race was still sometimes an issue:

> ... although you are a student and obviously had the requirements to be on the course they still maybe treat you differently to another student that is on the same placement, or even a year behind you. They expect you to know a bit less ... so you are always proving yourself which makes your load double the normal load. And yet it wasn't the same with the lecturers; they interviewed you, they gave you that place on the course. They know you deserve to be there so lecturers were never a problem, but fellow students always were a bit like that, always.

We saw that Patricia described herself as 'an academic'; she came to the UK imbued with a strong learner identity and sense of her academic abilities. The adherence between the field and her habitus and cultural capital meant that this identity was transferable and viable in the UK and gave her narrative a sense of coherence. Similarities between the two educational systems in terms of the learning culture and expectations, and the absence of a language barrier smoothed her transition to learning in the UK. Patricia's experience of higher education was similar to her formal learning experiences in Zimbabwe, and she was able to confidently draw upon the knowledge, experience and practices she had accumulated, and apply them to learning in the UK. Being able to capitalise on her existing capitals and convert them into symbolic capital and power meant that when she was confronted with a difference – the more individualised nature of learning in the UK – she had the confidence and security to address them by trying to set up a discussion group. Bourdieu uses the term doxa to describe the immediate adherence or 'taken for granted' sense between a habitus and the field to which it is attuned (Bourdieu, 1977:164).

In contrast, Farideh, who came from a very different education system, had struggled to construct her identity as a learner in the UK. She was recognised and recognised herself as not having much cultural value.

Institutional mechanisms had fixed the value of her capital and inculcated a belief in that value, to the extent that she could not occupy the social space with any degree of entitlement or belonging. She was constantly aware that she didn't have the 'right' knowledge and experienced this as feeling out of place, and suffering constant doubt and insecurity about her ability to succeed in higher education. What Bourdieu referred to as the 'feel for the game' or the 'almost miraculous encounter between the habitus and a field, between incorporated history and an objectified history ...' (1990:66) was absent.

After three years in higher education (one year at Masters level and two at undergraduate level), Farideh would still refer to differences in the teaching and learning styles and expectations. Towards the end of her four year degree she said she felt that learning 'was becoming easier', although she still worries that she might fail and have to re-sit exams, even though she has never failed a course. She says she finds it harder to concentrate when studying and to revise for exams than she used to in Iran, although she puts this down to growing older rather than to the trauma or stress associated with migration or the ongoing struggle of being in a social field in which her capital and habitus is not recognised.

Farideh had not established meaningful relationships during her time as a student. The daily commute gave her little opportunity to establish friendships and studying in London was an isolating and lonely experience. While studying locally she had made friends with other refugees on the WILAW course, particularly one of the other students from the course who went on to do a degree at the same university:

> Sometimes we go to library together, the silent area. I like it when he's sitting and writing all the time so I don't talk to him and he doesn't talk to me ... he studies, I study and then we go for a cup of tea. It's good to know somebody in the uni, because I don't know many people there, so when I see him it's something familiar.

In contrast, she felt she had not made friends during the first two years of her degree course:

> At the moment there is just one lady, originally from Sri Lanka ... We haven't got anything in common but just age. So sometimes we talk together but not with other students. The younger students like to be together ... I tried to say hello to them but the day after they didn't know me.

Her cultural habitus distanced and differentiated Farideh from other students. There was no sense of shared everyday practices with other students. She didn't, for instance, go to bars or drink alcohol. There was no sign of ease or belonging which comes from occupying a social space with others who have a similar habitus. Both Alan's and Savalan's narratives emphasise the alternative positive identities and sense of moral worth provided by being a student. Like Farideh, however, neither have the sense of ease, the 'fish in water' quality that characterises the interactions of students (or indeed any group) with similar habitus. They had very different understandings and expectations of family, and the economic realities in which they live and which constrain and shape their lives generated distinction. Their past, the history and experience of being a refugee, distanced them from fellow students. In short, their habitus was indelibly marked by their refugee background, creating boundaries of belonging.

Alan and Savalan were both studying degrees which linked to their roles before they came to the UK: Alan as a civil engineer and Savalan in business. Importantly, both were able to draw upon their previous experiences and the knowledge they had accumulated and use it in their new identity as student. Despite differences in habitus, their cultural capital was perceived as legitimate and tradeable. Savalan believed that on his Access to business course and again in his university degree, his professional experience of working in Iran had helped him and given him confidence:

> Like, at first I was frightened a bit, you know. I didn't talk much because I felt because of my English language, you know? I knew that I knew more than them, but the way that I wanted to say and the way that they said was completely different. I mean the use of language. So I knew the idea but I could not say it ... It was like all the time, during my lectures, ... I was remembering marketing in my country or my business, you know just helping me a lot. You know because of that I knew all ideas, you know, things in business and stuff.

Similarly, Alan found that although he initially struggled with the language, to his relief studying at university was easier than he had anticipated and he could draw upon the calculations and the methods he had used in Iran on his MSc. The same was true for Maryam – in the first year of her degree in mathematics education she could draw upon and utilise her previous experience, although the second year was much harder as it involved educational and professional practices which were very different in the UK. For these three participants, the ability to draw upon their experiences and cultural capital seems to have been significant in easing their transition through the structures and expectations of higher education.

The use and acknowledgement of life experiences has been shown to be an important factor for working class students also, as they negotiate higher education (Merrill, 2007). Contradictions and tensions between learners' social and cultural background and the expectations and culture of higher education have been apparent. For example, tensions between working class affinities and identifications and the university have been a particular focus of attention (see Bowl, 2003; Bamber and Tett, 2000; Merrill, 2007; Quinn, 2004). Feminist researchers have also pointed out the obstacles faced by women students as they try to adapt to a context which privileges masculine ways of learning and knowing (eg. Morley, 1999; Quinn, 2003).

Much of this research points to the need to rethink institutional and pedagogical practices to reflect the increasingly diverse student population in higher education. In their review of widening participation research in higher education, Gorard *et al* (2006) call for a move away from the prevailing model of non-traditional students as being 'in deficit' and therefore requiring additional and separate provision to rectify perceived weaknesses. Instead, these authors argue, higher education institutions need to change, and support should be embedded throughout them. To this we might add a pedagogy which follows a Freirean model and recognises and builds upon the experiences, knowledge and professional skills which refugees bring with them into higher education. Here, the role of the educator is not to by-pass what individuals bring with them in terms of their understanding of the world; on the contrary, it is to recognise and to respect their knowledge and understanding. This 'local' or 'partial' context is the base from which other knowledge can be constructed (Freire, 1992).

This shift from the individual learner to institutional and pedagogical practices involves, in Bourdieu's terms, conceptualising higher education as a cultural field (or set of fields), and encourages reflection on what is currently privileged and valued in these fields and what fails to be recognised or legitimised. Rather than seeing particular students as 'inferior' and lacking the right kinds of cultural capital or academic skills, the gaze shifts to what would need to be recognised if higher education was to develop a stronger focus on equity. This perspective encourages attention to the measures at a curricular or pedagogical level which might support the successful integration of refugees into higher education. As suggested in Farideh's narrative, for example, making explicit and transparent the requirements of assessment modes such as the essay, and recognising that such dominant practices are conflicting and contested across higher education.

In their research on academic literacy practices in higher education, Lea and Street (1998) showed how greatly academic expectations varied across higher education institutions, courses and even individual tutors. Assumptions about the nature of knowledge affected the meaning given to terms such as 'structure', 'evidence' and argument', giving rise to variations and contradictions in the academic writing expected. Lea and Street concluded that:

> ... elements of successful student writing are in essence relating to particular ways of constructing the world and not to a set of generic writing skills as the study skills model would suggest. (1998:163)

The outcomes of higher education as an education strategy to establish a positive identity and accrue tradeable capital were mixed for these students. Although studying gave Alan a sense of subjective well-being, he was unable to capitalise on the qualifications achieved for employment reward. For the others, the cultural capital they accrued through education has enabled them to trade in the employment field. Significant for all was their refugee identity; this had marked their habitus and clearly identified them as different from other students. This is further complicated when refracted through the lenses of ethnicity and gender. Whether the higher education field enabled students to establish a positive learner identity depended on the extent to which it conferred legitimacy and value on their habitus and capital, and the consequent degree of entitlement and belonging they experienced.

11

Conclusions

Becoming a refugee involves managing unexpected changes in one's life trajectory and embarking on a journey to construct a viable identity and positive subjectivity in a new context. The decision to leave is often very sudden and occurs under circumstances over which they have little control. The events which precipitated their flight and the journey to the UK are stressful and traumatic. These can have long lasting, although not always visible, effect on their lives, their well being and ability to integrate.

This book offers a fine grained analysis of the migration process of people who have sought refuge in the UK. It presents migrants as social beings with particular attributes: gender, social class, ethnicity, parental status, age, religion, culture and stage in the life cycle. Each of the five individuals has their own unique biography which shapes and informs how they construct themselves. At the same time the processes of learning they experienced, which involve both deconstruction and reconstruction, draw upon, and are shaped by, broader discourses. Their narratives thus illuminate the interplay of structural forces, identity and agency.

I have argued that powerful ideologies and discourses essentialise the characteristics of refugees, positioning them as lacking the qualities needed to be good or successful citizens. The early narratives as asylum seekers presented by these five refugees illuminate the conflict between the ideal or imagined identities which they hoped to create, and the reality of an identity which positions them as excluded from economic, educational and other positive identity resources. This conflict produces coping strategies: in order to provide for themselves in the UK and not be dependent on welfare, they are forced to work in informal and semi-legal employment. Asylum seeking and refugee communities have developed relevant stores of knowledge and social capital which can be drawn upon to access such employment. Although this was a source of shame for all who had taken this route, it was also a source of agency, enabling them to resist the negative social positioning imposed by social policy and the powerful discourses surrounding asylum seekers and refugees.

The difference in entitlements and security between the status of asylum seeker and of refugee makes the status of refugee greatly preferable. Yet being a refugee was a humiliating identity, something to be kept hidden. While symbolic representations and negative stereotypes have a limiting and damaging influence on refugees' subjectivities and prevent them from generating positive valuations of themselves, they also provide a point of resistance against which the research participants struggled to construct positive identities and opportunities for self definition. Alternative discourses of working hard, being a good citizen, caring, studying and contributing to society are evident in the narratives of them all. They construct and present their identities in relation to difference from other refugees and in opposition to dominant discursive practices. A considerable amount of moral boundary work is directed at striving to construct and present themselves as having value and moral worth. We saw, for example, how Patricia converts what could be perceived as demeaning care work into a positive and respectable caring identity. Also, how Alan marks space between himself and others who share the same Kurdish and refugee identity, but who were not as committed as he was to learning English and integrating into his new country.

While migration subjected these refugees to loaded discourses and limiting social positioning, it simultaneously opened up opportunities for exploring alternative social practices, particularly in relation to gender. For both Farideh and Maryam migration offered a loosening of traditional gender roles and the possibility of learning and adopting a different kind of gender performance. There were fewer restrictions placed on their movements as women and on the identities they could take up. Nonetheless, race and ethnicity were important identity markers in all of the stories and it could be argued that as gender became de-emphasised, race became privileged and gained greater prominence as an identity signifier for Farideh, Maryam and Patricia.

A broad range of learning processes and practices were evident in the lives of participants. Many activities that would not normally be defined as learning and which were not part of any formal learning structures, provided valuable learning opportunities. They learned English through television and the internet, for example, and learned through observing, absorbing and interacting with the social life around them. All had a strong desire to socialise and learn; they recognised the importance of learning in informal contexts and through mixing with non-refugees.

Through social activity and interaction, these refugees constructed meaning and learned the social identity of refugee. All had faced hostility and racism in their daily lives, which affected subjectivities and feelings of belonging. Learning what it means to be a refugee and their place in UK society was not always positive: much learning is profoundly disturbing, involving, as it does, the unlearning of self and learning what you can no longer be. Conceptualising learning as a response to life events and involving the ongoing de- and re- construction of self illuminates these processes of subjective reconstruction. In Bourdieu's (1977; 1998) terms, this learning is concerned with ongoing symbolic struggles to prove and gain acceptance for capitals. It is also an attempt to be recognised as having moral worth (Sayer, 2005; Skeggs, 1997).

Refugees are firmly placed into symbolic structures of inequality, determining what economic and educational opportunities are available to them and limiting their access to different forms of capital. The participants were structured and positioned through mechanisms of capital transformation and trading which meant they had few opportunities to convert and trade up the capitals they possessed into symbolic capital, and educational and employment reward. Each was from a habitus which brought particular dispositions and which framed expectations and behaviours in the new social space. For most of them the process of reconstructing themselves in the UK involved trying to re-establish a professional identity and finding employment in the same or similar profession. Alongside this, they also struggle to be seen as worthy of respect. The store of social and cultural capital which had enabled them to achieve educational and professional status in their own country was generally not recognised and valued in the UK and could not be converted into symbolic capital.

All of them saw higher education as a route to re-establishing a professional identity. How this occurred and the ease with which educational success could be achieved largely depended on the extent to which their capital could be deployed, and the degree of adherence between their habitus and the field in question. This was illuminated in Patricia's case: the English colonial education system of Zimbabwe had not only equipped her with the English language skills which, even in Zimbabwe, were recognised as being an advantageous capital, but also the 'essayist literacy practices' required for success in the UK higher education system (Lillis, 2001). In higher education she was able to operate with security and confidence which having the right kind of knowledge and capital instils. She had a sense of entitlement and belonging to social space which enabled her to effectively trade up through education into symbolic capital and educational reward. For the others, whose capitals were not as mobile and were not accepted, access to higher education meant not only improving and developing their English language skills, but also adapting to the new and unfamiliar expectations of the field. Farideh was acutely aware that her forms of capital were judged to have little value. Her cultural habitus as an Iranian woman placed her in a subordinate position because it marked her out as a student of inferior quality, unprepared for the expectations of higher education. She experienced higher education as anxiety, insecurity and feeling out of place. Denied opportunities for capital transformation and trading, the transition and the construction of a confident learner identity was more difficult and has taken longer.

Attempts to rebuild their lives through the UK education and qualification system did not succeed for those who lacked the power to convert the cultural capital they had achieved into symbolic capital. We noted Alan's disappointment when he realised that his Masters in civil engineering did not have exchange value and could not be traded up for employment reward. In a labour market where notions of 'people like us' are still influential in hiring practices, his social positioning as a refugee and the ethnic markers of his habitus acted as codes of distinction to classify him as different and inferior. Excluded from the formal labour market, Alan was prevented from capitalising upon his newly acquired cultural capital.

Schemes of perception and classification are deeply embedded in public discourses and the labour market is no different. Employment sectors hold entrenched cultures and expectations around which certain groups are best suited for particular jobs. These give rise to unfair and discriminatory practice yet they are difficult to challenge and shift. Injustices of this kind are exposed by recent research conducted by the Refugee Council (2010b). Funded by the Training and Development Agency for schools, the research looked at the experiences of refugee teachers who wish to gain Qualified Teacher Status (QTS) in the UK. There are two main routes for an overseas trained teacher (OTT) to gain Qualified Teacher Status (QTS). One is through the Post Graduate Certificate in Education (PGCE), the other is via employment-based initial teacher training programmes. In order to access the latter route, the teacher has to be employed by a school, which can then support their application for the Overseas Teacher Programme.

The Refugees into Teaching project found that where refugee OTTs were able to find work in schools it was largely through supply agencies, rather than directly through the schools. Approximately 72 per cent of OTTs working as unqualified teachers in England are employed through supply agencies. Consequently, these agencies play a central role as gatekeepers to OTTs looking for work. The vast majority of OTTs working as unqualified teachers in England are from Australia, Canada and New Zealand (69%); most are young and on the two year Youth Mobility Scheme introduced in 2008.

The Refugee Council research found that embedded within these agencies was a culture which selected and prioritised teachers from these 'traditional' countries, rather than teachers from countries which refugee teachers come from. Compared to this 'traditional' group of OTTs, refugee teachers struggled to find work in schools. Priority was given on grounds of nationality rather than experience, subject knowledge and teaching ability. The agencies tended to recruit and supply the OTTs which schools expected, and had been happy with in the past.

The effect of this was to restrict the range and length of teaching placements for refugee OTTs to the occasional day of supply work rather than longer term contracts. This is turn meant that the opportunity to teach in their subject specialism was limited, there were few opportunities to adapt to the English system or demonstrate their pedagogical skills, and their role in schools was seen as temporary – which inhibited opportunities to build relationships within the school.

The overall consequence is that very few refugee OTTs have the opporunity to work for four years as an unqualified teacher and gain QTS through the employment-based route. So widespread was the view that certain nationalities make better teachers, that even Zimbabwean OTTs, despite being fluent in English and often having studied for UK accredited qualifications, are under-represented as OTTs working in schools. The experience of Refugees into Teaching is that the majority of refugee OTTs who gain QTS do so through the PGCE route (Refugee Council, 2010b).

Patricia and Alan had taken the British citizenship test and applied for a British passport. Under the five year rule, Savalan was not entitled to apply for British citizenship until one year after he had applied for, and been granted, Settlement Protection (Indefinite Leave to Remain). For both, adopting the identity of British citizen was for instrumental and pragmatic purposes, rather than affective reasons of wishing to belong or feelings of inclusion. For Patricia, it was primarily to facilitate her mother's visit to the UK. For Alan, it was to make it easier to travel outside of the UK and to improve his employment prospects. Becoming a British citizen was therefore about the perceived membership rights and benefits it would entail. The existence of family members all over the world gave a multi-layered complexity to feelings of home and belonging. Thoughts of return to a home country fluctuated over time, as conceptualisations of the past changed in the light of present circumstances.

Implications and lessons for policy and practice

Contemporary society is characterised by ever increasing movements of people around the globe – including the movement of refugees. This process is evidenced by rapid and visible social and cultural change in communities. Many communities in the UK are now 'super-diverse', characterised by a plethora of different minority groups living side by side (Vertovec, 2006). Globalisation of the economy inevitably involves the globalisation and the interdependence of people, yet this challenge of diversity is not reflected in current lifelong learning policy priorities. Indeed, as discussed in chapter three, current constructions of lifelong learning focus ever more tightly on the perceived needs of the economy, that is, on individual skills development, and are less and less concerned with opportunities to gain greater cultural awareness and understanding and to explore critically what it means to be a citizen in a global world (see eg. Biesta, 2006; Field, 2006; Burke and Jackson, 2007; Jarvis, 2006b). The essentially humanistic concerns set out in earlier seminal reports such as the Faure Report (1972), or the four pillars of learning set out by Delors and colleagues: learning to be, learning to do, learning to live together and learning to know (Delors, 1996), have increasingly become occluded in current discourses.

Yet the narratives presented here indicate that these broader learning agendas may well be more relevant than ever before. Learning to live with different cultural or social world views and values is a collective challenge requiring collective learning responses – learning which brings people together and opens up spaces for dialogue, rather than pursuing the individualised and instrumental approach currently dominating policy. More appropriate would be a pedagogy which supports personal and social development and provides opportunities for considering different world views and cultural practices. Importantly, it requires recognition of the often hidden affective dimension of not only becoming a refugee but also of adapting to a new culture.

In its *Memorandum on Lifelong Learning* (2000), the European Commission recognises that European societies are 'turning into intercultural mosaics' and that in this complex social and political world we need to 'learn to live positively with cultural, ethnic and linguistic diversity' (2000:5). The report consequently suggests that the joint aims of lifelong learning in Europe are to promote employability and active citizenship. However, a closer look at what is meant by 'active citizen' reveals not only a focus on participation in the social life of the country and the extent to which individuals feel they belong, but also a further reiteration of 'employability' which it defines as 'a core dimension of active citizenship' (2000:3).

Yet the findings of my research indicate that employability was not generally the issue for this group of refugees; participants managed to find employment working in care homes, the security industry, catering, cleaning and other low paid, low status areas of work. The twin concerns for participants were to rebuild and re-establish their professional lives and identities and, closely allied, to re-generate a sense of respectability and value in themselves as moral subjects. Policy does little to support refugees in this respect. As we have seen, it has more often worked to stymie opportunities for capital trading and to reinforce their symbolic derogation.

This is probably most clearly to be seen while asylum seekers are waiting for a decision on their claim. Unable to work, they are forced to either depend on state benefits or work illegally. Both routes make it virtually impossible to maintain a sense of dignity and self respect, or to utilise their skills and experience. In their Let Them Work Campaign the Refugee Council has highlighted the inhumanity and distress caused by denying asylum seekers the right to work. The more recent policy of restricting the access of asylum seekers to English language classes (LSC, 2006) has also become the subject of campaigns, involving ESOL practitioners, Trade Unions and groups working with refugees. For Alan, isolated, lonely and suffering from depression, English language classes were a lifeline while he was dispersed to Birmingham, yet this sanctuary would be unavailable to those in a similar position today. Being able to attend English language classes, and having the opportunity to meet other people, is fundamental to the process of starting to rebuild lives. The impact of legislation granting only temporary refugee status (Home Office, 2005) is highlighted in Savalan's narrative. We saw how his temporary status was increasingly influencing his decision making and his ability to apply for employment at the end of his degree. These policies are disempowering, as they make it more difficult for refugees to imagine and plan for a future for themselves in the UK.

Brine (2006) argues that European policies around lifelong learning can be viewed in terms of a structural hierarchy of learners. Learners are constructed within two discernable discourses: a discourse of the knowledge economy, which consistently relates to higher level graduate learners; and a discourse of the knowledge society, linked to discourses of social cohesion and political stability, which is concerned with learners who have low skills or who are unemployed. The latter are the gendered, classed and 'raced' learners needing basic and social skills training. Education and training initiatives for this latter group are more concerned with ensuring social and political stability than enabling them to develop high level skills for the knowledge economy.

In response to increasing concerns about social cohesion, the UK Government introduced citizenship classes for refugees (see chapter two). Refugees must either pass an ESOL with citizenship test, or if their language is Entry level three or above, a Knowledge of Life and Language in the UK test. Citizenship classes are designed to promote knowledge of life in the UK and the shared values necessary for successful integration. I have critiqued this narrow understanding of social inclusion, citizenship and integration elsewhere (Morrice, 2007). It is a 'top down' approach to learning and citizenship, whereby values, identities and understandings are determined by the Government, rather than by opening up spaces for individuals to actively engage in developing their own identities and sense of citizenship or belonging. Such policy initiatives are arguably underpinned by an agenda of social and moral regulation, an agenda which is further reinforced by the citizenship test which refugees wishing to apply for British citizenship must now pass. Although abandoned because they were felt to be too complicated, the more recent notion of 'earned citizenship' suggest that this is the direction in which policy is likely to continue moving.

Despite the high level of skills and aspiration expressed by refugees, policy appears to position them firmly in what Brine (2006) called the discourse of the knowledge society. They have not been included in the discourse of the knowledge economy which relates to the up-skilling and development of higher level graduate learners. Rather than highlight the forms of capital, experience and skills that could contribute to and enrich society, policy has instead positioned refugees firmly in the social cohesion and stability discourses: a problem to be contained and managed, rather than an asset or resource to be developed.

At the same time, and in recognition of the needs of modern developed economies, the UK Government has introduced a points-based system to manage migration and ensure that business and employers have access to the skills the economy needs. The result is that Governments in the global north are able to select the most skilled and educated workforce from the global south. Policy which has a more globally sensitive vision would acknowledge the damage to low income countries caused by the continual harvesting of sections of its workforce, and would instead shifts its gaze to the potential of the workforce on its own doorstep. The question then becomes: how can we create the conditions to develop the human potential that is here and willing to be mobilised?

Including refugees in the discourses of the knowledge economy would entail ensuring access to the mechanisms and social sites where they could trade their capital, develop assets and apply them within the new context. Some of the practical measures needed came through in the case studies: for example, the need for individualised and specialised advice and guidance on how to top-up and build upon qualifications gained overseas. There is recognition that refugees with professional skills and experience require specialist advice (Home Office, 2006b; Houghton and Morrice, 2008), and that this might not be available from statutory employment agencies such as JobCentre Plus, whose role it is to support people from welfare into work.

In its employment strategy for refugees, the Department for Work and Pensions (DWP) acknowledged that JobCentre Plus did not have the expertise to deliver the degree of specialist help needed by refugees (DWP, 2005). Although the problem was recognised, subsequent policy has done little to address it. The Consultation Paper for a New Model for National Refugee Integration Services in England (Home Office, 2006b) proposed a specialist service for 'professional' refugees, but these proposals were dropped by the time the more recent integration strategy for refugees was published in 2009 (Home Office, 2009b). Instead the new strategy comprises a Refugee Integration and Employment Service (RIES), which aims to get 30 per cent of refugees into work within a year of receiving status. Funded by the UK Border Agency and delivered regionally, it initially offered up to twelve months support, including employment advice focusing on achieving job readiness, and a mentoring service based on the Time Together mentoring framework (see chapter six). The strategy does not specify that refugees should be supported into employment commensurate with their skills and experience – rather it is about any available employment.

Funding cuts meant that the level of support available through this service was reduced in September 2010 and is due to be cut completely in autumn 2011. Yet for many refugees, the first months after receiving their status are, as we have seen, spent sorting out urgent practicalities such as welfare benefits and housing, and improving their language skills. It can take months and even years before they are in a position to start rebuilding their careers. If refugees are to utilise and build upon their existing qualifications and skills they need a service offering specialist advice, which can be accessed at any point.

Research has identified the need for specialised, advanced language provision, such as English for academic or vocational purposes (see Houghton and Morrice, 2008; Morrice, 2009a). Government funded English language classes are only available up to level two. Higher level language classes to equip people for academic or professional fluency are generally restricted to fee paying students. Public funding for International English Language Testing System (IELTS) courses for example, was withdrawn in 2008 (LSC, 2007). This internationally recognised test of English language proficiency is a requirement for entry to UK universities. It is also a pre-requisite for entering certain professions, for instance it is required by the General Medical Council in order to register to practice medicine. The cost of preparing for the exam and then the cost of the test is a significant and often insurmountable barrier for refugees.

Since August 2007 refugees who are not receiving income-based benefits are no longer entitled to free English language courses at any level. Refugees moving into areas of employment requiring low level communication skills could consequently become trapped in these areas. Denying refugees the opportunity to develop higher level language skills will have the inevitable effect of further restricting the range of employment that they can access and the benefits they might bring to society.

Higher education offers refugees a key route for capitalising on existing skills and qualifications, and qualifying for access to professional and skilled employment. However, gaining access and meaningful participation was difficult and at times problematic. Getting qualifications recognised and gaining access to university is the first hurdle. Refugees with overseas qualifications at a higher level need to have brought their degree certificates with them, or manage to have them sent to the UK. If they cannot prove their qualifications they normally have to start a degree again. Those who can produce a degree certificate must have their qualification assessed by the National Recognition Information Centre for the UK (UKNARIC). This provides a UK equivalent to their overseas qualification. In the majority of cases degrees are assessed as being below Batchelor Honours degree level, which means that refugees are likely to have to return to university but, hopefully, with appropriate guidance, to top up their degree rather than start at the beginning.

In 2008 the Government introduced the policy of Equivalent and Lower Qualification (ELQ). The aim was to prioritise funding for students taking a degree for the first time and meant that students who already had an equivalent or higher qualification to the one they were applying for would not be eligible for Government funding (with a few exceptions, such as teacher training or medicine). At the time of writing, the Refugee Council is conducting research into the impact this policy is having on refugees. It appears that while their qualifications are being assessed at a lower level and they are therefore accepted as home students, they are being refused student loans for their fees. This is because eligibility for fee loans is calculated on the length of previous HE study and not only UK equivalence. The Refugee Council have pointed out that as a result a number of refugees have had to drop out of their degrees or find the money from other sources (Lee, 2010). We saw in the case studies that finances were a particular issue for refugees. Bank loans are not readily available without an established employment history of regular work, and as refugees are likely to be sending remittances to family members, they will not have the financial resources to fall back on should a loan not materialise. This oversight in policy making suggests that policy requires 'refugee proofing' to ensure that such distressing and negative impact is avoided.

Once in university, the refugee's qualifications, knowledge and professional expertise were often not recognised or given space for development. Institutional practices and processes, such as the privileged place of academic writing and the essay as a form of assessment, disadvantaged those from a habitus and cultural background who did not possess this privileged form of knowledge. Despite the increasing internationalisation and diversity of students in higher education, those without the 'right kinds of knowledge' still tend to be seen as being in deficit, and this is reflected in both pedagogy and practice (Gorard *et al*, 2006). The present research suggests the need for greater openness to different ways of knowing, and recognition of the way that refugees, and others from diverse social backgrounds, can contribute to the development of new knowledge and new ways of seeing the world.

This research has also drawn attention to the limitations of learning. As it shows, successful completion of a university degree is no guarantee of employment. Examples of direct and indirect discrimination faced, for example, in the labour market are sobering reminders that education alone cannot solve intractable social issues such as prejudice and injustice. Despite this caveat, the recent *Inquiry into the Future for Lifelong Learning* highlights the role learning can have in helping citizens to deal creatively and constructively with situations of social diversity and uncertainty (Schuller and Watson, 2009). The authors make two recommendations pertinent to refugees and to how lifelong learning can contribute to social cohesion. Drawing on Raymond Williams' three roles of lifelong learning in times of rapid change – to make sense of change, to adapt to change and to shape change – and to Amatyr Sen's notion of capabilities, they propose a citizens' curriculum. They recommend that all citizens have access to opportunities to develop their capabilities in four areas: digital, health, financial and civic. While steering clear of specifying the content, or the mode of learning, they propose a framework within which local initiatives and variants could be developed. Most relevant to my argument is their suggestion for a minimum local adult education offer which would guarantee access to learning in relation to each of the four capabilities.

Such an initiative, as long as it is kept broad enough to respond to diverse local needs, has the potential to draw learners from different social backgrounds, refugee and non-refugee, and provide a space in which understanding of culture and self could be explored and developed, both formally and informally. The inquiry also proposes a 'welcome entitlement' to anyone moving into a new locality, be they internal migrants or from overseas. The idea is to give the incomer a chance to make social contact with the community and to contribute to social capital and social cohesion. Both these initiatives are to be welcomed. They have the potential to move beyond the current learning silos which keep refugees in a narrow range of prescribed learning, and to bring people together across traditional boundaries. The authors point out that educational venues are one of the main surviving public spaces where people from diverse backgrounds come together as active participants in a joint venture (Schuller and Watson, 2009).

There is clearly a huge amount of work still to be done to change attitudes and perceptions around asylum issues, and to support refugees to demonstrate their skills and the myriad ways they have enriched and contributed to UK culture and society. The UK has a long history of providing sanctuary to people fleeing persecution, stretching back to the seventeenth century French Huguenots. It is a proud history, and one which in the current political climate needs to be reclaimed and celebrated.

Final reflections

Refugees are not a homogeneous group. Characteristics such as social class, gender and ethnicity all impact upon and shape the experience of being a refugee, as of course does country of origin and education background. The journeys and struggles related in this book are those of refugees who come from particular social and economic class backgrounds, and their values, beliefs and goals reflect these backgrounds. The stories of refugees from poor and socially disadvantaged backgrounds who have not had the privileges of education or training in the country they have come from are missing. Research is needed to capture the lives, struggles and contributions to UK society of this group.

This book aims to provide rather more than a snapshot of the experiences of refugees. It has sought to paint a more holistic picture: one which depicts refugees as individuals who had vibrant lives, and belonged to families and communities before they became refugees, and to give an account of how becoming a refugee changed their lives and how, over time, they negotiated new, liveable lives. What has become clear is that the identity and learning processes which accompany migration are ongoing and iterative. These are stories of constant flux and of ongoing journeying and struggle, rather than arrival. The process is not linear and has no clearly identifiable start or end point. Although my study followed their lives for five years, the narratives represent only a fragment, albeit a crucial one, of the lives of these refugees. How the past and present will come together in the future is part of that ongoing journey.

Bibliography

Abrahamian, E. (1992) *The Iranian Mojahedin.* London, Yale University Press

Ager, A. and Strang, A (2004) *Indicators of Integration: Final Report.* London, Home Office

Al-Ali, N. (2007) *Iraqi Women. Untold stories from 1948 to the present.* London, Zed

Aldridge, F. and Waddington, S. (2001) *Asylum Seekers Skills and Qualification Audit Pilot Project.* Leicester, NIACE

Alheit, D. (2005) Stories and structures: An essay on historical times, narratives and their hidden impact on adult learning. *Studies in the Education of Adults*, 37(2), 201-212

Alheit, P. and Dausien, B. (2002) The 'double face' of lifelong learning: Two analytical perspectives on a 'silent revolution'. *Studies in the Education of Adults*, 34(1), 3-22

Alheit, P. and Dausien, B. (2007) Lifelong learning and biography: A competitive dynamic between the macro- and the micro- level of education. In: West, L., Alheit, P., Siig Andersen, A., and Merrill, B. (Eds.) *Using Biographical and Life History Approaches in the Study of Adult and Lifelong Learning: European perspectives. (vol. 2).* Frankfurt am Main, Peter Laing

Al-Khalil, S. (1989) *Republic of Fear. The politics of modern Iraq.* Berkley and Los Angeles, University of California

Armstrong, P. F. (1987) *Qualitative Strategies in Social and Educational Research: The life history method in theory and practice.* New land papers, University of Hull

Ball, S. J. Maguire, M. and Macrae, S. ((2000)) *Choice, Pathways and Transitions Post-16: new youth, new economies in the global city.* London, RoutledgeFalmer

Bamber, J. and Tett, L. (2000) Transforming the learning experiences of non-traditional learners: A perspective from higher education. *Studies in Continuing Education*, 22(1), 57-75

Bauman, Z. (2004) *Wasted Lives. Modernity and its outcasts.* Cambridge, Polity Press.

Beck, U. (1992) Risk Society. London, Sage

Bertaux, D. (1981) *Biography and Society: the life history approach in the social sciences.* London, Sage

Biesta, G. J. J. (2006) *Beyond Learning. Democratic education for a human future.* Boulder, Paradigm Publishers

Bloch, A. (2002) *Refugee's Opportunities and Barriers in Employment and Training. Report for Department for Work and Pensions.* DWP, Leeds

Bloch, A. (2007) Refugees in the UK labour market: The conflict between economic integration and policy-led labour market restriction. *Journal of Social Policy*, 37(1), 21-36

Bloch, A. (2008) Zimbabweans in Britain: transnational activities and capabilities. *Journal of Ethnic and Migration Studies*, 34(2), 287-305

Bloch, A. and Schuster, L. (2005) At the extremes of exclusion: deportation, detention and dispersal. *Ethnic and Racial Studies*, 28(3), 491 – 512

Bloomer, M. (1997) *Curriculum Making in Post-16 Education: the social conditions of studentship.* London, Routledge

Bloomer, M. and Hodkinson, P. (2000) Learning careers: continuity and change in young people's dispositions to learning. *British Educational Research Journal*, 26(5), 583-598

Bloomer, M., and Hodkinson, P. (2002) Learning careers and cultural capital: adding a social and longitudinal dimension to our understanding of learning. In: Nata, R. (Ed.) *Progress in Education.* (vol. 5). Hauppauge NY, Nova Science

Borg, C., and Mayo, P. (2005) The EU memorandum on lifelong learning. Old wine in new bottles? *Globalisation, Societies and Education,* 3(2), 203-225

Boshier, R. (1998) Edgar Faure after 25 years: down but not out. In: Holford, J., Jarvis, P. and Griffin, C. (Eds.) *International Perspectives on Lifelong Learning.* London, Kogan Page

Boud, D., Keogh, R. and Walker, D. (Ed.) (1985) *Reflection: turning experience into learning,* London, Croom Helm

Bourdieu, P. (1977) *Outline of a Theory of Practice.* Cambridge, Cambridge University Press

Bourdieu, P. and Wacquant, L.J.D. (1992) *An Invitation to Reflexive Sociology.* Cambridge, Polity Press

Bourdieu, P. (1998) *Practical Reason.* Cambridge, Polity Press

Bourdieu, P. (1999) The contradictions of inheritance. In: Bourdieu, P., Accardo, A., Balazs, S., Beaud, F., Bourdieu, E., Bourgois, P., Broccolichi, P., Champagne, R., Christin, J.P., Fageur, S., Garcia, R., Lenoir, F., Oeuvrard, M., Pialoux, M., Pinto, L., Podalydes, D., Sayad, A., Soulie, C., Wacquant, Loic J.D. (Eds.) *Weight of the World: social suffering in contemporary society.* Cambridge, Polity Press

Bourdieu, P. (2004) The forms of capital, in: S. Ball (Ed.) *Reader in Sociology of Education.* London, RoutledgeFalmer

Bowl, M. (2003) *Non-traditional Entrants to Higher Education. 'They talk about people like me'.* Stoke on Trent, Trentham Books

Brine, J. (2006) Lifelong learning and the knowledge economy: Those that know and those that do not – the discourse of the European Union. *British Educational Research Journal*, 32(5), 649-665

Burke, P. J. and Jackson, S. (2007) *Reconceptualising Lifelong Learning. Feminist interventions.* London, Routledge

Candappa, M. and Egharevba, I. (2002) Negotiating boundaries. Tensions within home and school life for refugee children. In: Edwards R. (Ed.) *Children, Home and School. Regulation, autonomy or connection?* London, RoutledgeFalmer

Castles, S. (2003) Towards a sociology of forced migration and social transformation. *Sociology*, 37(1), 13 -34

Castles, S. and Kosack, G. (1973) *Immigrant Workers and Class Structure in Western Europe.* Oxford, Oxford University Press

Castles, S., and Miller, M. (2003) *The Age of Migration. International population movements in the modern world, (3rd edn).* Basingstoke, Palgrave Macmillan

Chamberlayne, P. Bornat, J. and Wengraf, T. (2000) *The Turn to Biographical Methods in Social Science.* London, Routledge

Chappell, C., Rhodes, C., Solomon, N., Tennant, M. and Yates, L. (2003) *Reconstructing the Lifelong Learner. Pedagogy and identity in individual, organisational and social change.* London, RoutledgeFalmer

Coffield, F. (2000b) A critical analysis of the concept of a learning society. In: Coffield, F. (Ed.) *Differing Visions of a Learning Society. (vol. 1).* Bristol, Policy Press

Coffield, F. (Ed.) (2000a) *The Necessity of Informal Learning.* Bristol, The Policy Press

Colley, H., Hodkinson, P. and Malcolm, J. (2003) *Informality and Formality in Learning: A Report for the Learning and Skills Research Centre.* London, Learning and Skills Research Centre

Commission of the European Communities (2000) *Commission Staff Working Paper. A Memorandum on Lifelong Learning.* Brussels, EC

Crossan, B., Field, J., Gallacher, J. and Merrill, B. (2003) Understanding participation in learning for non-traditional adult learners: Learning career and the construction of learning identities. *British Journal of Sociology of Education*, 24(1), 55-67

Crowther, J. (2004) 'In and against' lifelong learning: Flexibility and the corrosion of character. *International Journal of Lifelong Education*, 23(2), 125-136

Davies, B. (2006) Identity, abjection and otherness: Creating the self, creating difference. In: Arnot, M., Mac an Ghaill, M. (Eds.) *The RoutledgeFalmer Reader in Gender and Education.* London, Routledge

Davis, E. (2005) *Memories of State. Politics, history, and collective identity in modern Iraq.* London, University of California Press

Delors, J. (1996) *The Treasure Within: Report to UNESCO of the international commission on education for the twenty-first century.* Paris, UNESCO

Department for Business Innovation and Skills (BIS) 2010) *Investing in Skills for Sustainable Growth* (Strategy Document FE-New Horizons). London, BIS

Department for Education and Skills (DfES) (2007) Race Equality Impact Assessment on Proposed Changes to the Funding Arrangements for English for Speakers of Other Languages and Asylum Seeker Eligibility for LSC Funding – Report and Emerging Proposals. http://rwp.excellencegateway.org.uk/readwriteplus/bank/ACF1BE9.pdf (Accessed January 2011)

Department for Work and Pensions (2005) *Working to Rebuild Lives: Refugee Employment Strategy.* Sheffield, DWP

Dominice, P. (2000) *Learning from our Lives; using educational biographies with adults.* San Francisco, Josey-Bass

Dumper, H. (2002) *Missed Opportunities. A skills Audit of Refugee Women in London from the Teaching, Nursing and Medical Professions.* London, Report for Greater London Authority

Edwards, R., Usher, R (1998) Lo(o)s(en)ing the boundaries: from 'education' to 'life-long learning'. *Studies in Continuing Education*, 20(1), 83-103

Faure, E. (1972) *Learning To Be: The World of Education Today and Tomorrow.* Paris, UNESCO

Field, J. (2005) *Social Capital and Lifelong Learning.* Bristol, Policy Press

Field, J. (2006) *Lifelong Learning and the New Educational Order.* Stoke-on-Trent, Trentham Books

Flynn, D. (2005) New borders, new management: The dilemmas of modern immigration policies. *Ethnic and Racial Studies,* 28(3), 463-490

Fraser, W. (1995) *Learning from Experience: empowerment or incorporation?* Leicester, NIACE

Freire, P. (1985) *The Politics of Education. Culture, power and liberation.* Westport, Bergin and Garvey

Freire, P. (1992) *Pedagogy of Hope.* London, Continuum

Freire, P. (1996) *Pedagogy of the Oppressed.* (M. B. Ramos, Trans.) London, Penguin

Giddens, A. (1991) *Modernity and Self Identity: self and society in the late modern age.* Cambridge, Polity

Gorard, S., Smith, E., May, H., Thomas, L., Adnett, N. and Slack, K. (2006) *Review of Widening Participation Research: assessing the barriers to participation in higher education.* Bristol, HEFCE

Griffin, C. (2002) Lifelong learning and welfare reform. In: Edwards, R., Miller, N., Small, N. and Tait, A. (Ed.) *Supporting Lifelong Learning. Vol 3, Making policy work.* London, RoutledgeFalmer

Griffiths, D., Sigona, N. and Zetter, R. (2005) *Refugee Community Organisations and Dispersal. Networks, resources and social capital.* Bristol, Policy Press

Hall, S. (1992) The question of cultural identity. In: Hall, S., Held, D. and Mcgrew, A. (Eds.) *Modernity and its Futures.* Oxford, Polity Press in association with Blackwells

Hall, S. (2000) Who needs 'identity'? In: Du Gay, P., Evans, J., and Redman, A. (Eds.) *Identity: a reader.* London, Sage

Hammerton, A. J. and Thomson, A. (2005) *Ten Pound Poms. Australia's invisible migrants.* Manchester, Manchester University Press

Hobson, C., Cox, J. and Sagovsky, N. (2008) *Saving Sanctuary. The Independent Asylum Commission's First Report of Conclusions and Recommendations.* London, IAC

Hodkinson, P., Ford, G., Hawthorn, R. and Hodkinson, H. (2007) *Learning as Being, Working Paper 6.* Report for Learning Lives Website. Http://www.learninglives.org. (Accessed April 2007).

Home Office (1999) *Immigration and Asylum Act.* London, HMSO

Home Office (2000) *Full and Equal Citizens.* London, Home Office

Home Office (2001) *Community Cohesion: A Report of the Independent Review Team.* Chaired by Ted Cantle. London, Home Office

Home Office (2002a) *Nationality, Immigration and Asylum Bill.* London, HMSO

Home Office (2002b) *Secure Borders, Safe Haven: Integration with Diversity in Modern Britain. White Paper.* London, The Stationery Office

Home Office (2004) *Asylum and Immigration (treatment of claimants, etc) Act.* London, HMSO

Home Office (2005a) *Integration Matters: A National Strategy for Refugee Integration.* London, Home Office

Home Office (2005b) *Controlling Our Borders: Making Migration Work for Britain. Five Year Strategy for Asylum and Immigration.* London, Home Office

Home Office (2006a) *Immigration, Asylum and Nationality Act (IAN).*London, HMSO.

Home Office (2006b) *A New Model for Refugee Integration Services in England: Consultation Paper.* London, Home Office

Home Office Border and Immigration Agency (2008) *The Path to Citizenship: Next Steps in Reforming the Immigration System.* London, Home Office

Home Office (2009a) *Control of Immigration: Statistics United Kingdom 2009.* Http://rds.Homeoffice.Gov.Uk/rds/pdfs10/hosb1510tabs.Xls (Accessed October 2010). London, Home Office

Home Office (2009b) *Borders, Citizenship and Immigration Act 2009.* London, HMSO.

Home Office UK Border Agency (2009a) *Moving on Together: Government's Recommitment to Supporting Refugees.* London, Home Office

Home Office UK Border Agency (2009b) *Earning the right to stay – a new points test for citizenship.* London, Home Office

Honarbin-Holliday, M. (2008) *Becoming Visible in Iran. Women in contemporary Iranian society.* London, Taurus Academic Studies

Houghton, A. M. and Morrice, L. (2008) *Refugees, Asylum Seekers and Migrants. Steps on the education and employment progression journey.* Leicester, NIACE

Jacobsen, K. and Landau, L. B. (2003) The dual imperative in refugee research: Some methodological and ethical considerations in social science research on forced migration. *Disasters,* 27(3), 185-206

Jarvis, P. (2006b) Beyond the learning society: globalisation and the moral imperative for reflective social change. *International Journal of Lifelong Education*, 25(3), 201-211

Jarvis, P. (2006a) *Towards a Comprehensive Theory of Human Learning.* Oxon, Routledge

Johnson, N. (2007) Building an integrated society. In: Wetherell, M., Lafleche, M. and Berkeley, R. (Eds.) *Identity, Ethnic Diversity and Community Cohesion.* London, Sage

Jonker, B. (2004) *Resource Project Refugee's Contribution to Europe. Country report: UK.* London, RETAS

Keddie, N. R. (2003) *Modern Iran. Roots and results of revolution,* (Updated edition). London, Yale University Press

King, K. P. (1999) *Changing languages, cultures and self: the adult ESL experience of perspective transformation.* Http://www.adulterc.org/proceedings/1999/99King.pdf. (Accessed March 2009)

Kirk, R. (2004) *Skills Audit of Refugees. Home Office Online Report 37/04.* Http://www.Homeoffice.Gov.Uk/rds/pdfs04'rdsolr3704.Pdf. (Accessed March 2005). London, Home Office

Knowles, M. (1970) *The Modern Practice of Adult Education: andragogy versus pedagogy.* Chicago, Follett Publishing Company

Kofman, E., Phizacklea, A., Rhahuram, P. and Sales, R. (2000) *Gender and Migration in Europe.* London, Routledge

Kolb, D. (1984) *Experiential Learning.* New Jersey, Prentice Hall

Kundnani, A. (2001) In a foreign land: The new popular racism. *Race and Class*, 43(2) 41-60

Lave, J. (1996) Teaching, as learning, in practice. *Mind Culture and Activity*, 3(3), 149-165

Lave, J. and Wenger, E. (1991) *Situated Learning: legitimate peripheral participation.* Cambridge, Cambridge University Press

Lea, M. R., and Street, B. V. (1998) Student writing in higher education: An academic literacies approach. *Studies in Higher Education*, 23(2), 157- 172

Lee, J. (2010) Personal correspondence with James Lee, Employment and Training Policy Advisor, Refugee Council. See also Freedom of Information request and answer submitted by Lee and available at: http://www.whatdotheyknow.com/request/refugee_affected_by_the_equivale?post_redirect= (Accessed January 2011)

Learning and Skills Council (2006) *Raising our Game. Our Annual Statement of Priorities (October 2006).* Http://readingroom.lsc.gov.uk/lsc/National/nat-annualstatementofpriorties-reoct2006.pdf. (Accessed February 2009).

Learning and Skills Council (2007) *Our Statement of Priorities. Better Skills, Better Jobs, Better Lives. The LSC's priorities and key actions for 2008/9 to 2010/11.* Http://readingroom.Lsc.Gov.Uk/lsc/national/nat-statementofpriorities-nov07.Pdf. (Accessed November 2010)

Lillis, T. M. (2001) *Student Writing. Access, regulation, desire.* London, Routledge.

Lynn, N. and Lea, S. (2003) 'A phantom menace and the new apartheid': The social construction of asylum seekers in the United Kingdom. *Discourse and Society*, 14(4), 425-452

Martin, I. (2003) Adult education, lifelong learning and citizenship: some ifs and buts. *International Journal of Lifelong Education*, 22(6), 566-579

McGregor, J. (2007) 'Joining the BBC (British bottom cleaners)': Zimbabwean migrants and the UK care industry. *Journal of Ethnic and Migration Studies*, 33(5), 801-824

Merrill, B. (2007) Recovering class and the collective in the stories of adult learners. In: West, L., Merrill, B., Alheit, P., Bron, A., and Siig Andersen, A. (Ed.) *Using Biographical and Lifehistory Approaches in the Study of Adult and Lifelong Learning.* Frankfurt-am-Main, Peter Lang

Merrill, B. and West, L. (2009) *Using Biographical Methods in Social Research.* London, Sage

Mezirow, J. (1990) *Fostering Critical Reflection in Adulthood: A guide to transformative and emancipatory learning.* San Francisco, Jossey-Bass

Mezirow, J. (2000) *Learning as Transformation.* San Francisco, Jossey-Bass

Morley, L. (1999) *Organising Feminisms: The micropolitics of the academy.* Hampshire, Macmillan Press

Morrice, L. (2005) Lifelong learning and the 'outsider': The case of refugees and asylum seekers in the UK, paper presented at the *Diversity and Difference in Lifelong Learning. The Proceedings of the 35th Annual Conference of SCUTREA: Standing Conference on University Teaching and Research in the Education of Adults, University of Sussex, UK* 5-7 July 2005

Morrice, L. (2007) Lifelong learning and the social integration of refugees in the UK: the significance of social capital. *International Journal of Lifelong Education*, 26(2), 155-172

Morrice, L. (2009) Journeys into higher education: the case of refugees in the UK. *Teaching in Higher Education*, 14(6), 663-674

Plummer, K. (2001) *Documents of Life 2. An invitation to a critical humanism.* London, Sage

Plumridge, L. and Thomson, R. (2003) Longitudinal qualitative studies and the reflexive self. *International Journal of Social Research Methodology*, 6(3), 213-222

Portes, A. (2004) A cross-Atlantic dialogue: The progress of research and theory in the study of international migration. *International Migration Review*, 38(3), 823-51

Putnam, R. D. (2000) *Bowling Alone: The collapse and revival of American community.* New York, Simon and Schuster

Quinn, J. (2003) *Powerful Subjects: are women really taking over the university?* Stoke-on-Trent, Trentham

Quinn, J. (2004) Understanding working-class 'drop-out' from higher education through a sociocultural lens: cultural narratives and local contexts. *International Studies in Sociology of Education*, 14(1), 57-74

Rapley, T. (2001) The art(fulness) of open ended interviewing: Some considerations on analysing interviews. *Qualitative Research*, 1(3), 303-323

Refugee Council (2009) *Joint Parliamentary Briefing from the British Refugee Council, the Scottish Refugee Council and the Welsh Refugee Council: Borders, Citizenship and Immigration Bill 2009.* http://www.refugeecouncil.org.uk/Resources/Refugee%20 Council/downloads/parliamentary_briefings/BCI%20brief%20update%20-%20May% 2009.pdf (Accessed December 2010)

Refugee Council (2010a) *Applying for permission to work while claiming asylum. Refugee Council Briefing, October 2010.* http://www.refugeecouncil.org.uk/ Resources/Refugee%20Council/downloads/briefings/permission%20to%20work%20 briefing%20oct2010 (Accessed January 2011)

Refugee Council (2010b) *Policy Briefing on Refugee overseas trained teachers: experiences of employment and initial teacher training.* http://www.rit.refugeecouncil.org. uk/sites/default/files/OTT%20Finding%20and%20Recommendations%20RiT%20- %20final.pdf (Accessed January 2011)

Robinson, V. (2003) Defining the problem. In: Robinson, V., Andersson, R. and Musterd, S. (Ed.) *Spreading the Burden? A review of policies to disperse asylum seekers and refugees.* Bristol, Polity Press

Rogers, C. (1967) *On Becoming a Person.* London, Constable

Rogers, C. (1980) *A Way of Being. Boston.* Houghton Mifflen Company

Sales, R. (2007) *Understanding Immigration and Refugee Policy. Contradictions and continuities.* Bristol, Policy Press

Sanasarian, E. (1992) The politics of gender and development in the Islamic Republic of Iran. In: Jabbra, J. G. and Jabbra, N. W. (Eds.) *Women and Development in the Middle East and North Africa.* New York, E. J. Brill

Sayer, A. (2005) Class, moral worth and recognition. *Sociology*, 39(5), 947-963

Schon, D. (1983) *The Reflective Practitioner.* New York, Basic Books

Schon, D. (1987) *Educating the Reflective Practitioner.* San Francisco, Jossey-Bass

Schuller, T. and Watson, D. (2009) *Learning through Life. Inquiry into the future for lifelong learning.* Leicester, NIACE

Sfard, A. and Prusack, A. (2005) Telling identities: In search of an analytic tool are investigating learning is a culturally shaped activity. *Educational Research*, 34(4), 14-22

Skeggs, B. (1997) *Formations of Class and Gender.* London, Sage

Somerville, W. (2007) *Immigration under New Labour.* Bristol, Policy Press

Stevenson, J. (2008) 'Always on the outside, always looking in': Ethnic minority women's experiences of exclusion from higher education communities of practice, paper presented at the *European Society for Research into Education of Adults. Access, Learning Careers and Identities Network Conference, Educational Journeys and Changing Lives*, 10-12 December 2008. University of Seville, Spain

Thomson, A. (2003) *Life histories and educational research and practice.* Seminar presentation, Centre for Continuing Education, University of Sussex 23 September 2003

United Nations (2009) *Trends in International Migrant Stock: The 2008 Revision* (United Nations Database, pop/db/mig/stock/rev.2008). Http://esa.un.org/migration/p2k0data.asp. (Accessed October 2010)

United Nations High Commissioner for Refugees (UNHCR) (2006) *The State of the World's Refugees: Human Displacement in the New Millennium.* Oxford, Oxford University Press

United Nations High Commissioner for Refugees (UNHCR) (2007a) *Convention and Protocol Relating to the Status of Refugees.* Geneva, UNHCR. Http://www.Unhcr.Org/3b66c2aa10.Html. (Accessed July 2010)

United Nations High Commissioner for Refugees (UNHCR) (2007b) *Refugee Protection and Durable Solutions in the Context of International Migration. Report on the High Commissioner's Dialogue on Protection Challenges, December 2007.* Http://www.Unhcr.Org/cgi-bin/texis/vtx/search?Page=search&docid=47fe0e532&query=dpc. (Accessed September 2010)

United Nations High Commissioner for Refugees (UNHCR) (2010) *2009 Global Trends. Refugees, Asylum Seekers, Returnees, Internally Displaced and Stateless Persons. Division of Programme Support and Management.* Http://www.unhcr.org/4c11f0be9.pdf. (Accessed September 2010)

Usher, R., Bryant, I. and Johnston, R. (2002) Self and experience in adult learning. In: Harrison, R., Reeve, F., Hanson, A., Clarke, J. (Eds.) *Supporting Lifelong Learning. Vol 1. Perspectives on learning.* London, RoutledgeFalmer

Vertovec, S. (2006) *The Emergence of Superdiversity in Britain, working paper no. 25.* Oxford, Centre on Migration, Policy and Society

Waddington, S. (2005) *Valuing Skills and Supporting Integration.* Leicester, NIACE

Wenger, E. (1998) *Communities of Practice. Learning, meaning and identity.* Cambridge, Cambridge University Press

West, L. (1996) *Beyond Fragments: adults, motivation and higher education; a biographical analysis.* Abingdon, Taylor and Francis

West, L. (2001) *Doctors on the edge. General practitioners, health and learning in the inner city.* London, Free Association Books

West, L., Alheit, P., Siig Andersen, A. and Merrill, B. (2007) *Using Biographical and Life History Approaches in the Study of Adult and Lifelong Learning: European perspectives.* Frankfurt am Main, Peter Laing.

Wetherell, M. (2007) Community Cohesion and Identity Dynamics: Dilemmas and challenges. In: Wetherell, M., Lafleche, M. and Berkeley, R. (Eds.) *Identity, Ethnic Diversity and Community Cohesion.* London, Sage

Wight Mills, C. (1959) *The Sociological Imagination.* New York, Oxford University Press

Yu, E.S.H. and Liu, W. T. (1986) Methodological problems and policy implications in Vietnamese refugee research. *International Migration Review,* 20(2), 483-501

Yuval-Davis, N., Anthias, F. and Kofman, E. (2005) Secure borders and safe haven and the gendered politics of belonging: Beyond social cohesion. *Ethnic and Racial Studies*, 28(3), 513 – 535

Zetter, R. (2007) More labels, fewer refugees: Remaking the refugee label in an era of globalisation. *Journal of Refugee Studies*, 20(2), 172-19

Index